S0-AZP-866

⋯⋯> CREATING A HEALTHY SCHOOL

USING THE | # Healthy School Report Card *2nd Edition*

SUSTAINABLE
FORESTRY
INITIATIVE

Certified Fiber Sourcing

www.sfiprogram.org

an ASCD ActionTOOL

CREATING A HEALTHY SCHOOL

USING THE

Healthy School Report Card

2nd Edition

ASCD
LEARN. TEACH. LEAD.
Alexandria, Virginia USA

1703 North Beauregard St. • Alexandria, VA 22311-1714 USA
Phone: 1-800-933-2723 or 1-703-578-9600 • Fax: 1-703-575-5400
Web site: www.ascd.org • E-mail: member@ascd.org
Author guidelines: www.ascd.org/write

Gene R. Carter, *Executive Director;* Judy Zimny, *Chief Program Development Officer;* Judy Seltz, *Chief Constituent Services Officer;* Nancy Modrak, *Publisher;* Sean Slade, *Director, Healthy School Communities;* Adriane N. Tasco, *Project Manager, Healthy School Communities;* Mary Beth Nielsen, *Director, Editorial Services;* Alicia Goodman, *Project Manager;* Gary Bloom, *Director, Design and Production Services;* Greer Wymond, *Senior Graphic Designer;* Mike Kalyan, *Production Manager;* Keith Demmons, *Desktop Publishing Specialist;* Sarah Plumb, *Production Specialist*

© 2010 by ASCD. All rights reserved. This publication is intended for professional development by the purchaser and authorized staff, who may photocopy limited portions for noncommercial distribution to authorized staff only. All other use, reproduction, and distribution of the action tool is strictly prohibited without prior written permission from ASCD. Contact Rights & Permissions via our website at www.ascd.org.

Printed in the United States of America. Cover art © 2010 by ASCD. ASCD publications present a variety of viewpoints. The views expressed or implied in this book should not be interpreted as official positions of ASCD.

All web links in this book are correct as of the publication date below but may have become inactive or otherwise modified since that time. If you notice a deactivated or changed link, please e-mail books@ascd.org with the words "Link Update" in the subject line. In your message, please specify the web link, the book title, and the page number on which the link appears.

Quantity discounts for the paperback edition only: 10–49 copies, 10%; 50+ copies, 15%; for 1,000 or more copies, call 1-800-93302723, ext. 5634, or 1-703-575-5634.

PAPERBACK ISBN: 978-1-4166-1123-3   ASCD Product #110140   n10/10
PDF e-book ISBN:978-1-4166-1149-3

Library of Congress Cataloging-in-Publication Data
Lohrmann, David K.
  Creating a healthy school using the healthy school report card / David K. Lohrmann. -- 2nd ed.
    p. cm.
  Includes bibliographical references.
  ISBN 978-1-4166-1123-3 (pbk. : alk. paper)
 1. School health services--United States--Evaluation. 2. School health services--United States--Planning. 3. School children--Health and hygiene--United States. 4. School hygiene--United States. I. Title.
  LB3409.U5L64 2010
  371.7'1--dc22
                                                                  2010025239

17 16 15 14 13 12 11 10   10 9 8 7 6 5 4 3 2 1

USING THE | Healthy School Report Card *2nd Edition*

STEP 3: REPORTING

STEP 4: USING THE RESULTS

APPENDIX

Acknowledgments

Support for the research and development of the Healthy School Report Card was provided by a grant from The Robert Wood Johnson Foundation in Princeton, New Jersey.

Downloads

Electronic versions of the tools are available for download
at **www.ascd.org/downloads**.

Enter this unique key code to unlock the files:

G188E 07385 DBE1F

If you have difficulty accessing the files, e-mail webhelp@ascd.org
or call 1-800-933-ASCD for assistance.

ASCD © 2010. All Rights Reserved.

Electronic Tools and Resources

DOWNLOADABLE TOOLS

The tools and Healthy School Report Card are available for download. To access these documents, visit www.ascd.org/downloads and enter the key code found on page viii. All files are saved in Adobe Portable Document Format (PDF). The PDF is compatible with both personal computers (PCs) and Macintosh computers. The main menu will let you navigate through the various sections, and you can print individual tools or sections in their entirety. If you are having difficulties downloading or viewing the files, contact webhelp@ascd.org for assistance, or call 1-800-933-ASCD.

Minimum System Requirements

Program: The most current version of the Adobe Reader software is available for free download at www.adobe.com.

PC: Intel Pentium Processor; Microsoft Windows XP Professional or Home Edition (Service Pack 1 or 2), Windows 2000 (Service Pack 2), Windows XP Tablet PC Edition, Windows Server 2003, or Windows NT (Service Pack 6 or 6a); 128 MB of RAM (256 MB recommended); up to 90 MB of available hard-disk space; Internet Explorer 5.5 (or higher), Netscape 7.1 (or higher), Firefox 1.0, or Mozilla 1.7.

Macintosh: PowerPC G3, G4, or G5 processor, Mac OS X v.10.2.8–10.3; 128 MB of RAM (256 MB recommended); up to 110 MB of available hard-disk space; Safari 1.2.2 browser supported for MAC OS X 10.3 or higher.

Getting Started

Select "Download files." Designate a location on your computer to save the file. Choose to open the PDF file with your existing version of Adobe Acrobat Reader, or install the newest version of Adobe Acrobat Reader from www.adobe.com. From the Main Menu, select a section by clicking on its title. To view a specific tool, open the Bookmarks tab in the left navigation pane and then click on the title of the tool.

Printing Tools

To print a single tool, select the tool by clicking on its title via the Bookmarks section and the printer icon, or select File then Print. In the Print Range section, select Current Page to print the page on the screen. To print several tools, enter the page range in the "Pages from" field. If you wish to print all of the tools in the section, select All in the Printer Range section and then click OK.

HEALTHY SCHOOL REPORT CARD ONLINE ANALYSIS TOOL

The purchase of this manual entitles your school to unlimited access to the online analysis tool found on ASCD's Healthy School Report Card website at www.healthyschool communities.org/reportcard.

To access the online analysis tool, you must create a user ID and password. Go to www .healthyschoolcommunities.org/reportcard and complete the fields in the area for new users. You'll then receive an e-mail confirming your user ID and password. If you have any problems accessing the online analysis tool, please contact us at healthyschoolcommunities@ascd .org.

DISCUSSION AND COLLABORATION WEBSITE

The Healthy School Report Card has its own discussion and collaboration website dedicated to creating a healthy school community: www.ascd.org/healthyschoolcommunities. On this site, teams can search the database, review case studies, analyze research, and ask questions.

ASCD © 2010. All Rights Reserved.

Introduction

What Is Healthy School Communities?

Healthy school communities are settings in which students, staff, parents, and community members work collaboratively to ensure that each student is emotionally and physically healthy, safe, engaged, supported, and challenged. They are settings in which the school and community engage each other to effectively support the school improvement process.

Healthy School Communities (HSC) is part of multiyear plan to shift public dialogue about education from a focus on merely academics to a whole child approach that encompasses all factors required for successful student outcomes. HSC is built around

- **A belief in the whole child:** The belief that successful learners are emotionally and physically healthy, knowledgeable, motivated, and engaged.
- **Best practice leadership:** Best practices in leadership and instruction across the school.
- **Strong collaborations:** Creating and sustaining strong collaborations between the school and community stakeholders and institutions.
- **A systems approach:** Using evidence-based systems and policies to support the physical and emotional well-being of students and staff.
- **Environment:** Providing an environment and developing a school culture in which students can practice what they learn about making healthy decisions and staff can practice and model healthy behaviors.
- **Data:** Using appropriate data to continuously improve.
- **Networking:** Networking with other school communities to share best practices.

Every school has students who miss class because of physical health–related issues or students who cannot concentrate because of pain, discomfort, or physical injuries. Schools may have students who are preoccupied with conflicts at home; feel unsafe at school; or, for a variety of reasons, may not feel supported at school. Each and every one of these situations or

conditions impedes students' abilities to perform at their best and educators' abilities to teach most effectively.

Students who do not feel safe, supported, or connected to their schools and communities, for example, are more likely to be disengaged from activities in the classroom. Disengagement from class and school increases the likelihood that students will participate in a range of risk-taking behavior, be absent from school, and experience increasing levels of harassment, all of which lessen students' ability to excel at school. (Arthur, Brown, & Briney, 2006; California Department of Education, 1999; Castelli, Hillman, Buck, & Erwin, 2007; Centers for Disease Control and Prevention, 2006; Chomitz et al., 2009; Dwyer, Sallis, Blizzard, Lazarus, & Dean, 2001; Fiscella & Kitzman, 2009; Hanson, Austin, & Lee-Bayha, 2004; Hillman & Castelli, 2009; Murray, Low, Hollis, Cross, & Davis, 2007; Pyle et al., 2006; Sallis et al., 1999; Tomporowski, 2003; Tremblay, Inman, & Willms, 2000; Trost, 2007)

Preventable physical and mental health, safety, and well-being issues compromise the ability of a substantial number of students to master even the best-designed curriculum. Unless the school is a healthy, safe, engaging, supportive, and challenging place to be, many of the best school improvement initiatives will fall short. HSC addresses these issues by targeting a systemic and foundational approach to school health and school improvement.

HSC places health and well-being directly into the school and education arena. This is a departure from the traditional coordinated school health program, which allows health to be separate from many of the policies, practices, and processes of the school at large. The Healthy School Report Card is a school improvement tool that provides the means for schools to address both the needs of the whole child—to be healthy, safe, engaged, supported, and challenged—and the overall efficiency and coordination of the school site, policies, and processes.

ASCD © 2010. All Rights Reserved.

Figure 1 | Healthy School Communities and School Improvement

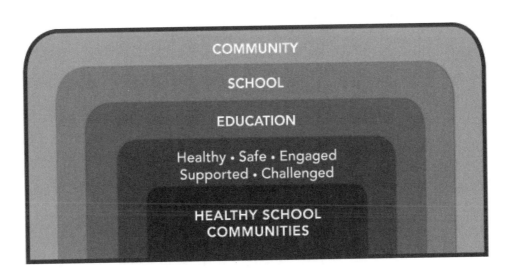

THE NEED FOR HEALTHY SCHOOL COMMUNITIES

According to the World Health Organization, a health-promoting school is a place where all members of the school community work together to provide students with integrated and positive experiences and structures that promote and protect their health. This includes both the formal and informal curricula in health, the creation of a safe and healthy school environment, the provision of appropriate health services, and the involvement of the family and wider community in efforts to promote health (World Health Organization, n.d.).

The World Health Organization's description incorporates the many structural factors that are part of each component of a coordinated approach to school health. Also known as a coordinated school health (CSH) program, this approach led to the development of the definition of a health-promoting school culture as one that enables, motivates, supports, and reinforces student and staff adoption of healthy behaviors. The keys to successfully implementing a high-quality approach are the common, crosscutting factors of policy compliance, strategic planning, and program coordination.

Historically, schools have dealt with student health and well-being issues through standard hygiene classes, with in-school counseling, or by requiring immunizations prior to students entering school. Within schools, administrators handle—personally or through delegation—a range of issues related to health, safety, and well-being. Besides the links among health, well-being, and student outcomes mentioned earlier, many schools are also obligated to comply with legal health requirements. Frequently these include the following:

- Mandatory health instruction.
- Mandatory physical education classes.
- School well-being policies.
- School crisis response policies.
- School policy as it relates to student safety (including alcohol, tobacco, and other drug abuse; bullying and harassment; and violence and victimization).
- Safe and healthy physical environment standards.
- School maintenance of confidential student medical information.

Through the Healthy School Report Card process, HSC offers a practical strategy for structuring your school environment and creating a school culture that addresses the health and well-being of students and staff in evidence-based ways that support learning and teaching. Specifically, this action tool will help you

- Meet the guidelines and standards established by your state or provincial government.
- Meet the U.S. Department of Agriculture Local Wellness Policy requirements.
- Establish a school environment consistent with the World Health Organization's concept of health-promoting schools.
- Integrate best practices and methods of providing school health programming for a high-quality school.

The strategies in this tool are the result of data collected through school-community public health partners that participated in the Health in Education Initiative and from school and district research sites that used the Healthy School Report Card (see page 197 in the Appendix.). Consistently, schools stated that undertaking the processes outlined in the tool was as important as filling out the Healthy School Report Card itself. In contrast, schools that shortcut the processes reported that they did not have success in gaining staff and community support for their work once it was completed (Valois, 2009).

ASCD © 2010. All Rights Reserved.

The Purpose of the Healthy School Report Card

The Healthy School Report Card was developed from a traditional CSH framework, but it was expanded to suit and address the whole school improvement process. The Healthy School Report Card aims to improve schools across the classroom, staff room, cafeteria, and playground and into systemic policy levels. The primary functions of this tool are to assess your needs and create a school improvement path for your school. You can use the results from the Healthy School Report Card as the basis of a Healthy School Improvement Plan, which provides a path for making your school more efficient, effective, and healthy.

The Healthy School Report Card is the mechanism by which you can assess your schools' practices, identify and prioritize the changes that you can make, and incorporate the changes into your school improvement plan. The data you collect through the Healthy School Report Card will help you prioritize your school's needs and then address them through your school improvement plan, school wellness plan, or other systematic strategies. The many benefits of a planned, embedded healthy school culture will deepen the support for your school from policymakers, stakeholders, and the community.

The Healthy School Report Card process will help you

- Provide your school and the community it serves with tangible criteria for assessing factors linked to both student health and behavioral barriers to academic achievement.
- Make decisions that support the health and well-being of all students and staff and better enable students to achieve current academic goals and future life goals.
- Increase support among school administrators and decision makers for implementing an organizing framework to support student and staff wellness, student achievement, and family and community involvement.
- Report your school's support for student and staff wellness, positive student behavior, and academic achievement in conjunction with required academic reporting.

- Identify areas for improvement that you can integrate into your school improvement plan.

A major premise behind the tool is that school improvement hinges on broad-based assessment and planning across a variety of traditional and nontraditional measures within each setting, which is a unique school-community context.

To effectively address the physical, emotional, intellectual, and social problems of students and staff that can impede teaching and learning, HSC uses a coordinated approach that involves personnel, agencies, and programs—both in and out of the school. HSC seeks to effectively utilize, coordinate, and provide resources and processes to schools. This includes services for and resources from all participants: the students, the staff, and families and the local community.

The Healthy School Report Card process is designed to help you develop a healthy school culture, one that is broadly understood to encompass the safety, security, and quality of school facilities; the social and emotional climate within the school; the physical school environment; and multiple structural factors within each component of a CSH program. The combination and coordination of all characteristics is what maximizes the efficiency and effectiveness of the school and provides the optimal environment for successfully adopting additional curricula and programs. Schools cannot afford—in time, effort, or money—to continue to implement new programs and curricula without first addressing the school environment. That is, its structure, its climate, and its systems.

Through the Healthy School Report Card school and community, stakeholders can address fundamental school improvement issues that are barriers to learning, such as school climate and child and adolescent health, safety, and well-being. Research indicates that, by actively engaging and empowering schools and communities in the improvement process and by addressing health and well-being issues, schools have students who are healthier, more engaged, and more productive; attend class more frequently; and, when present, have clearer focus and perform better. (Aberg et al., 2009; Centers for Disease Control and Prevention, 2010a, 2010b; Coe, Pivarnik, Womack, Reeves, & Malina, 2006; Daley & Ryan, 2000; Dilley, 2009; Dwyer, Blizzard, & Dean, 1996; Dwyer, Coonan, Leitch, Hetzel, & Baghurst, 1983; Field, Diego, & Sanders, 2001; Haas & Fosse, 2008; Kim et al., 2003; Moran, 2008; Nelson & Gordon-Larson, 2006; Pelligrini & Smith, 1998; Shephard, 1996, 1997; Sibley & Etnier, 2003; Trost, 2009; Trudeau & Shephard, 2008; Vail, 2006a, 2006b; Viadero, 2008)

ASCD © 2010. All Rights Reserved.

THE HEALTHY SCHOOL REPORT CARD PROCESS

Schools vary widely in their support for school health and in the school health structures they have in place. Some schools offer the minimum, required services without coordination. Other schools have a high-functioning health or wellness team. This tool is designed to help all schools improve their health environments, regardless of their point along the continuum of school-community health programming. For schools that don't have a wellness team, this tool offers advice for establishing one; but it can also help energize an existing health or wellness team.

The action tool is designed for

- Schools that have an active, established wellness or health team.
- Schools that are beginning to establish a wellness or school health program.
- Schools that provide a variety of services to students but have not begun to coordinate efforts.
- Schools that have a wellness policy but do not have a school-based health or wellness team.
- Schools that have a health or wellness plan but have not integrated it into overall school improvement efforts.

Each of the four major steps in the process—and the tasks required for accomplishing each step—is described in detail in its own section. Each section of the tool also contains resources, references, and sample forms that will help you complete the work. The four steps in the Healthy School Report Card process are as follows:

Step 1: Organizing

This section will take you from garnering approval for using the Healthy School Report Card process in your school community, through establishing your wellness team and work groups, to developing a plan for completing the process.

Step 2: Scoring

This section includes the Healthy School Report Card and instructions for assessing your school community, inputting your responses into the online spreadsheet, and generating the data analysis and preliminary recommendations.

Step 3: Reporting

This section outlines how to interpret your data analysis report and how to share it with your work groups, decision makers, and the community stakeholders.

Step 4: Using the Results

This section discusses how to use the analysis of your data to focus on issues you can quickly address without additional resources and on strategies to incorporate longer-term issues into a school improvement plan, or Healthy School Improvement Plan.

In conjunction with these four steps, nine levers of change will enable you to most effectively use and implement the process. It is recommended that sites aim to follow all nine levers:

1. Planning teams should be principal-led.
2. Team leaders should aim to build a team to facilitate the process.
3. Team leaders should ensure that all stakeholders understand the value of their involvement.
4. Plans should address systemic issues at the school.
5. Plans should align with and be the basis of the overall school improvement process.
6. Plans should focus on those aspects revealed by the Healthy School Report Card assessment to have the most need.
7. Collaboration should commence from the start of the planning process.
8. Ongoing, purposeful professional development should be integrated to support the process.
9. School administration should actively seek out and access community resources.

In a 2009 Healthy School Report Card pilot-site evaluation, these levers were shown to be pivotal in catalyzing significant change in the culture of school communities.

Although the levers are consistent with school improvement literature, they diverge from the recommendations and practices promulgated by school health professionals for more than 20 years, particularly in regards to the role of the principal: Current school health professionals advocate for the health team to be led by a school health coordinator who is designated by the principal. However, the experiences of the pilot sites suggest that, when the principal led or co-led the HSC team, schools made greater strides and the HSC work was more fully and quickly embedded in the school improvement process than when the principal did not have a strong leadership role.

ASCD © 2010. All Rights Reserved.

UNDERPINNINGS AND CHARACTERISTICS OF THE HEALTHY SCHOOL REPORT CARD

The Healthy School Report Card consists of 11 characteristics that involve multiple, evidence-based indicators derived either from research findings or recognized best practices extracted from professional literature in general education, school health, public health, and medicine. The characteristics and indicators express commonly accepted standards for school programming that affect the physical, mental, emotional, social, and vocational health and safety of students and staff members. This second edition of the report card also reflects the standards for foods offered in schools put forth by the Institute of Medicine in 2007.

The characteristics and indicators are purposely limited to a select number of statements that describe the structural factors within the school that need to be present for

- Each characteristic to exist and function at a high level of quality.
- Health programming to be coordinated.
- Characteristics of a healthy school to be institutionalized.

All the indicators are essential to both health-promoting schools and high-performing schools, and each has the potential to positively affect the health and well-being of students and school staff members and reduce barriers to learning. The characteristics of the Healthy School Report Card are as follows:

1. **School Health Program Policy and Strategic Planning:** The school maintains a culture that supports health through compliance with comprehensive policies that address all aspects of a coordinated school health program. Key indicators include specific policies, professional development, policy monitoring and compliance, and strategic planning and evaluation.
2. **Coordination of School Health Programs:** The school culture facilitates coordination of all health programs to eliminate gaps and overlaps, expand access to health resources, and ensure high quality.
3. **Social and Emotional Climate:** The school social and emotional climate is conducive to students, families, and staff members feeling safe, secure, accepted, and valued. At the school level, indicators include expectations of students, student and family ownership, student bonding, and student conduct and discipline. At the classroom level, indicators involve instructional practice, tone, student self-management, and classroom management.
4. **Family and Community Involvement:** The school culture encourages, supports, and facilitates the involvement of parents and the broader community in health

programming. Key indicators encompass both family involvement and community involvement.

5. **School Facilities and Transportation:** The physical school environment involves buildings, grounds, and vehicles that are secure and meet all established safety and environmental standards. Indicators encompass safety and quality, security, and emergency management.

6. **Health Education:** The school culture strongly supports and reinforces the health literacy knowledge, attitudes, behaviors, and skills students learn through a high-quality curriculum. Key indicators include curriculum and instruction, structural supports, and assessment.

7. **Physical Education and Physical Activity:** The school culture strongly supports and reinforces the lifelong fitness knowledge, attitudes, behaviors, and skills students learn through a high-quality curriculum. Key indicators encompass curriculum and instruction, facilities, assessment, and opportunities for physical activity.

8. **Food and Nutrition Services:** The school culture supports, promotes, and reinforces healthy eating patterns and food safety for students, staff, and families. Key indicators include the quality of cafeteria food, support for healthy eating, availability of food in the school, and food safety.

9. **School Health Services:** The school culture ensures student access to primary prevention, intervention, and treatment of disease and medical disorders. Key indicators encompass staffing, basic services, and access to medical care.

10. **Counseling, Psychological, and Social Services:** The school culture ensures student access to primary prevention, intervention, and treatment of mental health and substance abuse problems. Key indicators include staffing, classroom support, support and intervention services, discipline-related intervention, and crisis management.

11. **School-Site Health Promotion for Staff:** The school culture ensures high-level job performance and healthy role models by supporting and facilitating the physical and mental health and well-being of all employees. Key indicators include health-promotion programming and an employee assistance program.

Achieving these standards at a high level should be the goal of every school community, and growth in one characteristic will often result in subsequent or corresponding growth in others. Even if each indicator only contributes a small amount, the combined contribution to health, well-being, student growth, and the development of a positive school climate and more efficient school will be substantial.

ASCD © 2010. All Rights Reserved.

The Purpose of the Healthy School Report Card

After completing the Healthy School Report Card, some schools, because of a lack of sufficient resources, find that they simply cannot address a number of indicators determined to either not exist or need improvement. In this case, reporting the needs identified by the report card can provide schools with the impetus for developing resources, programs, and policy. Community support for creating a healthy school can grow out of this work.

HEALTHY SCHOOL COMMUNITIES ECOLOGICAL MODEL

The model below shows how each of the Healthy School Report Card characteristics can work together to promote a healthy school, one that, over time, fully embeds all these characteristics into all of its processes, practices, and growth.

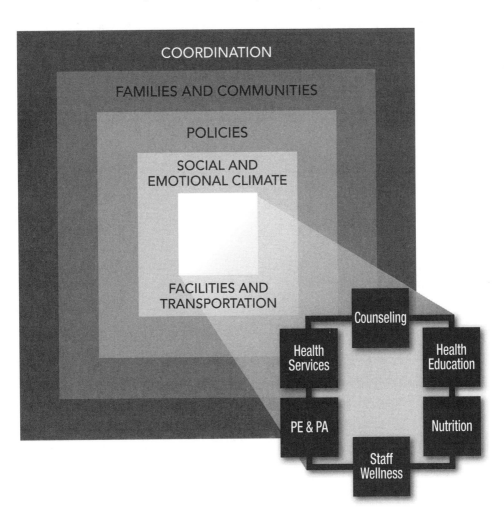

Integral to directly addressing student health and well-being, the core characteristics include designated, in-school health education, physical education, and established avenues for physical activity; access to essential health, counseling, psychological, and social services; and school-site health promotion for staff. Staff well-being directly influences student well-being, but it also affects school efficiency and long-term staff retention (Ciaccio, 2004; Cohen, McCabe, Michelli, & Pikeral, 2009; Hobson, Ashby, Malderez, & Tomlinson, 2009; Ingersoll & Kralik, 2004).

As illustrated by the box encasing these core characteristics, the entire school—the social, emotional, and physical environment—constitutes a climate and setting that supports the development of a healthy, safe, secure, and effective school. This type of school climate is created by responsiveness to the processes and practices taught across all subject areas, programs, and activities in the school setting.

Policies, which provide a guide and structure for school processes and practices, are vital for systemic change. The involvement of students' families and the community are also factors that influence student health and well-being and the efficiency and effectiveness of the school itself. The outer square, coordination, encompasses and cuts across all the characteristics into the core supports and services at the school.

ASCD © 2010. All Rights Reserved.

Key Understandings About the Healthy School Report Card

The Healthy School Report Card is a report card in the truest sense. The Healthy School Report Card is designed to provide a needs assessment of your school in regards to 11 characteristics. From this and subsequent ratings your HSC committee provides, the Healthy School Report Card process will provide a strategy your school should use as the basis for your school improvement plan. It does not provide an overall grade, nor is it designed to be seen as a pass-or-fail tool. The tool reports on your schools' progress and steps for growth.

The concept has become such an integral part of the school's identity that the staff integrated a detailed action plan into the school's improvement plan based upon our latest results from the Healthy School Report Card.

—*Jamie Buffington, Special Education Teacher, T. C. Howe Community High School, Indianapolis, Indiana, USA*

Each characteristic is essential and rated individually. Each indicator under every characteristic is treated separately based on three questions:

- Does it exist, and, if so, is the quality what it should be?
- How much benefit would accrue from undertaking efforts to improve it?
- How much effort would improving it require?

The combined answers to these questions determine whether that indicator needs to be addressed and, if so, its level of priority.

At first we thought it was going to be fresh fruits and vegetables and the snack—a healthy snack that we give our students—but it was more than that. It was looking at the whole child, the emotional, and the academic part of the child.

—*Angela Tuck, Principal, Edgewood Elementary School, Pottstown, Pennsylvania, USA*

The Healthy School Report Card helps schools identify areas for improvement and involve the community in the improvement process. The characteristics and indicators included in the report card express commonly accepted standards for school programming that affect the physical, mental, emotional, social, and vocational health of students and staff members. Achieving these standards at a high level should be the goal of every school.

The intent of the Healthy School Report Card is to assist school staff members, students, decision makers, and stakeholders in identifying indicators within their schools and districts that they can improve, given available resources. Some indicators that either do not exist or are in need of improvement may not be easy to address if you lack sufficient resources. However, during the school improvement planning process, community agencies may step forward to assist your school. When communities are welcomed and brought into the process from the beginning, they are more apt to provide support for developing health-promoting schools.

> *The strength of this structure is that when every stakeholder feels responsible for the success of the school, the community as a whole comes together to steward change and sustain culture. In this collaborative model, the entire community owns the culture.*
>
> —*Jacqueline Newton, Principal, Iroquois Ridge High School, Ontario, Canada*

The Healthy School Report Card does not require or provide a set of predefined actions. The report card provides clear results that outline both short- and long-term goals, recommends characteristics and indicators to focus on, and spotlights which indicators will require the most or least effort to achieve improvement. However, it is not a curriculum or a program. It intentionally does not provide a set of required or prescribed actions.

For schools and communities to truly create actions that will work for them, the people, organizations, and stakeholders of that community must come together to decide what is best. A fundamental understanding of HSC is that no two communities are the same, so what works in one school setting may not work in another. In fact, what works one year may not even have the same effect the following year.

For the Healthy School Report Card process to be truly authentic, it's important that each school-community team takes part in developing the subsequent school improvement plan and accompanying actions. Staff and stakeholders only truly become empowered and

ASCD © 2010. All Rights Reserved.

engaged in the process when it is *their* process. Each site team needs to develop and own its school improvement or Healthy School Improvement Plan.

The Healthy School Report Card is not a program; it is a process. Instead of imposing a one-size-fits-all curriculum or program, it allows—in fact, requires—each site to create a plan that suits its specific needs and aims. The path for this plan comes from the school's Healthy School Report Card results.

> We review the data monthly and, from the data, make decisions on whether we need to change our interventions or change what we are doing. We're not all the way there. We definitely have a long way to go. But our spring scores are amazing. And some of our kids have made two years' growth. They're really . . . flourishing, so that's impressive.
>
> —Carmen Dixon, Former Principal, Hills Elementary School, Iowa City, Iowa, USA

To help you gather information relevant to your individual situation, each characteristic of the report card includes a list of resources that can help you develop your own actions. In addition, the Healthy School Report Card has its own discussion and collaboration website (www.ascd.org/healthyschoolcommunities) dedicated to creating a healthy school community. On this site, teams can search the database, review case studies, analyze research, and ask questions.

The process is as valuable as the outcome. Although the systemic change to school policy, process, and practice is one key outcome for making schools healthier and more efficient, the process of achieving that change is equally important. The process includes gathering and garnering support, empowering stakeholders, establishing ownership, and structuring common language and purpose.

Empowering stakeholders creates a sense of ownership and increases the likelihood that improvements and discussion will be ongoing, even if a pivotal school-based leader, such as the principal, transfers or retires. The initial step in the Healthy School Report Card process, organizing (see page 23), sets the scene and builds trust and purpose to move discussions further. Some schools have found that the organization step is the most important and that the effort they put into it served them well in the subsequent steps.

The biggest thing that this initiative has done, for not just the school but the community as a whole, is really given everybody something they can buy into. I think it's always been something . . . under the radar—everybody knew how important school was; this just brought it out into the open.

—Justin Bennett, Union County Commissioner, New Mexico

ASCD © 2010. All Rights Reserved.

Healthy School Communities and the Whole Child

In 2007, ASCD formally stated its position on the whole child in *The Learning Compact Redefined: A Call to Action*:

> Current educational practice and policy focus overwhelmingly on academic achievement. This achievement, however, is but one element of student learning and development and only a part of any complete system of educational accountability. Together, these elements support the development of a child who is healthy, knowledgeable, motivated, and engaged. (p. 4)

ASCD believes that each child, in each school, in each of our communities deserves to be healthy, safe, engaged, supported, and challenged. We live in a time that requires our students to be prepared to think both critically and creatively, to evaluate massive amounts of information, solve complex problems, and communicate well, yet our education systems remain committed to time structures, coursework, instructional methods, and assessments designed more than a century ago.

The Whole Child Initiative plans to shift public dialogue about education from an academic focus to a whole child approach, moving from one in which students' achievement is measured solely by academic tests to one that considers students' knowledge, emotional and physical healthy, civic engagement, preparedness for economic self-sufficiency, and readiness for the world beyond formal schooling.

Healthy School Communities serves as an integral part of the Whole Child Initiative. The processes of the Healthy School Report Card provide a path for schools to address the needs of the whole child through the lens of health and well-being. It not only addresses the need for students to be healthy, but it also expands on traditional CSH programs by declaring that

students need to be safe, engaged, supported, and challenged. By means of HSC, schools are able to become whole child settings where the child is placed first.

ASCD © 2010. All Rights Reserved.

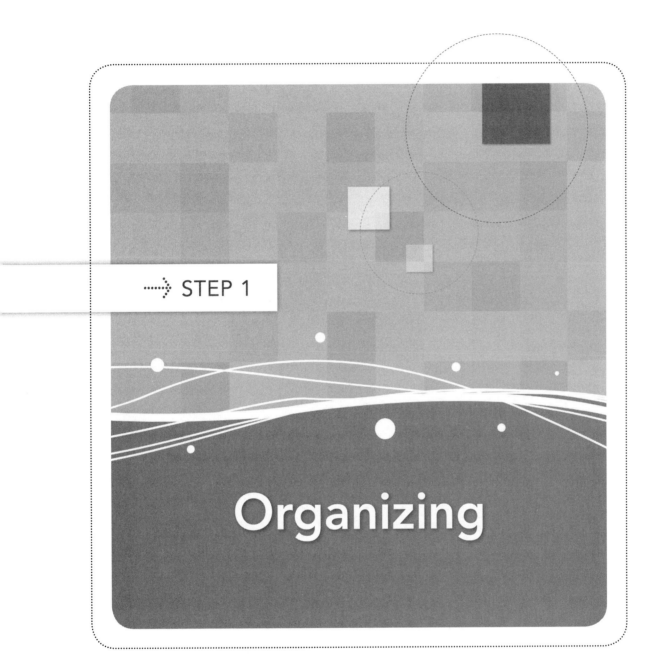

STEP 1

Organizing

Organizing for the Healthy School Report Card Process

Schools that have used the Healthy School Report Card—even those that already had a school health team in place—found that they were most successful if they took a few preparatory steps before beginning the assessment portion of the process.

Taking the time to get yourself and your leadership team organized could be the most important step you take. As noted in the introduction, the process of working through this action tool is as important as the outcome, and one cannot be separated from the other. Both accurate completion of the Healthy School Report Card and implementation of a Healthy School Improvement Plan require that those who participate in the scoring process (see Step 2 on page 61) are knowledgeable and fully engaged.

Those who have completed the Healthy School Report Card process advise three approaches that can be especially helpful:

1. **Identify parents** who are concerned about school improvement, health, and well-being issues and invite them to help you get organized.
2. **Involve students** as a way of accessing student voice and developing leadership and organizational skills.
3. **Invite and include local business or community leaders** who have a vested interest and who are well regarded in your community and who, through past activities, have well-established networks.

More often than not, schools are amazed at how willing school and community members are to participate once they are invited and part of authentic collaboration.

LAYING THE GROUNDWORK

If you do not have an established school health or wellness team, speak to your school administrator about the need to have a steering committee to assist with this work. Gather information on state, provincial, or national policies and guidelines that support or require a team to be put in place. Your state or province may have staff that can provide you with technical assistance and resources to help you in forming a team. Strategies for establishing a steering committee are outlined later in this section.

If you have an established school health or wellness team, use your regular communication and approval processes to garner administrative support for carrying out this assessment. Explicit support for this activity will enable you to access information and use your results in the school improvement process.

The activities that lay the groundwork for support are designed to

- Garner approval.
- Generate awareness.
- Help users manage expectations.
- Develop support and identify resources.
- Define at what level you will use your data.
- Plan how you will score the indicators.

Garnering Approval

Projects that include completing, assessing, and implementing data usually require prior administrative or board approval. Gaining formal approval (i.e., an administrative directive or school board resolution) is beneficial because such directives send a clear message to school staff and community members that creating a health-promoting school is an important objective. With approval in place, the team's work gains greater recognition among other staff and within the community.

Schools that have teams in place may not require additional approval for this work, but the most successful schools find that explicit administrative support is key to being able to complete the assessment activities. This approval will assist with your marketing and awareness activities and with data collection.

ASCD © 2010. All Rights Reserved.

Generating Awareness

Using the Healthy School Report Card data collection process not only informs stakeholders and decision makers about high-quality school health programs and services, but it also generates interest and support for health-promoting schools. For these benefits to accrue and for the process to go smoothly, it is imperative to inform decision makers and stakeholders about the Healthy School Report Card and how you will use the data well before it is actually implemented. You can share information through presentations at already scheduled meetings, individual meetings, telephone conversations, e-mails, electronic mailing lists, items in newsletters, and local media coverage.

Completing marketing and awareness activities ahead of time will widen the circle of support for the activity and help you avoid challenges. An effective marketing and awareness campaign also helps when recruiting individuals to assist with the process, because they will already be aware of your efforts when you contact them to request their participation. A good campaign is likely to stimulate interested organizations and individuals to volunteer to participate.

Managing Expectations

Sometimes school leaders are reluctant to use tools like this one because they are wary of raising expectations that they cannot meet. They feel that raising expectations that they believe they have no reasonable chance of meeting undermines their credibility. For example, some administrators are concerned that recommendations to improve facilities will face opposition within their community and that changes will not come to fruition.

The report card results do not dictate what must be done. However, the results will outline priorities and the extent to which you will need new resources to make short-term, midterm, and long-term changes. When you use this tool, you can manage others' expectations by

- Pointing out that, certainly, some changes in school health programming and services identified in the Healthy School Report Card data can be made. This is especially true of changes that require few new resources.
- Stipulating that some changes cannot be made without additional resources but that identifying those indicators in need of improvement can provide an opportunity for acquiring needed resources, especially from outside sources.
- Explaining that communities often step forward to undertake difficult challenges when given the opportunity.

In the final analysis, your school will choose to implement many of the recommendations identified by the Healthy School Report Card simply because they represent best professional practice. Using the results to inform the community about existing high-quality programming *and* pressing needs is an effective way to generate commitment, support, and resources from previously untapped sources.

Developing Support and Resources

Gathering information to complete the Healthy School Report Card requires allocating resources such as professional and support staff time, expertise, facilities, and supplies. Resources include staff time for planning, meeting, recording, and communicating; expertise related to skills such as organizing, data interpretation, and report writing; facilities such as office and meeting space; and supplies such as paper and photocopiers. Before beginning work on the Healthy School Report Card, identify the support and resources you need and where or how you will access them. Resources such as meeting space are often readily available in schools.

Defining the Level of Data Collection

Like many school improvement tools, this action tool is intended to be used primarily at the school level. This makes sense: although multiple schools within a district may share common characteristics, many important characteristics (e.g., social and emotional school climate) are specific to individual schools. However, some school districts may wish to compile data collected using the Healthy School Report Card at the district level or from within specified school clusters. Where data is compiled for a district or school cluster, all schools involved should undertake program implementation so that they can make changes, if needed, at both the school and district or cluster levels.

Planning

Successful outcomes for the Healthy School Report Card require planning at various points in the process. Planning that takes place prior to data collection will ensure that the scoring process moves smoothly and yields results that are accurate, meaningful, and actionable. Taking time to plan along the way will help your school achieve the end result of using the Healthy School Report Card.

ASCD © 2010. All Rights Reserved.

STRATEGIES FOR A SUCCESSFUL APPROACH

Because scoring can be a subjective process, with as many meanings and interpretations as there are stakeholders, you may find the following strategies helpful.

Appeal directly for honesty. Initially, and at intervals when working with your team members to complete the Healthy School Report Card, emphasize the spirit of the Healthy School Report Card, which is to work systematically to establish a health-promoting school culture for students and staff alike through honest, critical analysis and continuous quality improvement. The intent is not to make anyone look bad or to give the school a failing grade.

Involve external experts and consumers. External experts from the community and consumers of school health programs and services (i.e., students, family members, school staff members) should be included on the steering committee, on work groups that complete the various sections of the report card, and among those from whom you seek information. A recommended list of types of participants is included in the "Community Partners" tool on page 45.

Recognize existing, high-quality programming. Often completion of a status or needs assessment is viewed as a way of identifying and accentuating what is wrong with a school district or school. Another way to look at it is that completing a status or needs assessment is a way of identifying, accentuating, and crediting what is right with a school district or school. Point out that one purpose of completing of the Healthy School Report Card is to identify the positive aspects of school health programs and services that already exist.

Expose shortcomings in a constructive way. Sometimes we assume that those in charge of specific aspects of the school health program won't want shortcomings to be identified because doing so might make them or their schools look bad. In many instances, the individuals in charge are well aware of deficiencies that they have been unsuccessfully attempting to rectify or have intended to rectify. In other words, they are well aware of shortcomings and are not at all wary of exposing them. Point out that completing the Healthy School Report Card can actually provide the boost these individuals need to rectify shortcomings by drawing attention and assisting them with garnering the resources they need to effect change and improvement.

ASCD © 2010. All Rights Reserved.

Boost overall school quality. As noted in the introduction, academic achievement can be affected by health-related barriers to learning. Improvements to health programming spurred by use of the Healthy School Report Card can help schools address previously unrecognized barriers to learning that, when reduced or eliminated, can improve overall school quality. Emphasize that you cannot reduce or eliminate barriers to learning if those completing the report card are not willing to acknowledge that some indicators are not in place or, if in place, are not as effective as they could be.

Once you have completed the background work and received approval to use the Healthy School Report Card, the school health or wellness team can organize for data collection. The most successful mechanism for completing the work in this action tool is to use a steering committee to coordinate the activities and work groups to complete the Healthy School Report Card. Schools that have used the Healthy School Report Card indicate that the process outlined in this action tool is as important to gaining support for school health programming as the results they get from the report card.

ESTABLISHING A STEERING COMMITTEE

The process of selecting individuals to serve on your steering committee is a crucial step that affects the success of the entire process. Some schools use their existing school health or wellness teams or district school health council as a steering committee for this process. If you have an existing committee, review the membership to see if it is inclusive enough to accomplish the Healthy School Report Card process effectively. If you need to establish a team, the tools in this section can help you establish a steering committee.

Review the characteristics and indicators of the report card to identify the types of expertise that will benefit your work. Members should include

- Individuals within your school who have expertise in the different aspects of health and safety.
- Parents, community members, and health professionals who have interest and expertise.
- Student representatives.
- One or two individuals with high credibility among parents and the community (e.g., school board member, parent activist, physician, public health official, business leader, clergyperson) who will use their prestige to champion this effort.

ASCD © 2010. All Rights Reserved.

Ideally, members of the steering committee will also serve as chairs of the work groups that work on the 11 report card characteristics.

PLANNING FOR SUCCESS

Because the Healthy School Report Card is broken into distinct characteristics, some schools find it useful to form a separate work group for each characteristic. Ideally, each work group will be chaired by a member of the steering committee and include school staff with expertise in that area. For example, the school nurse or person who oversees the school clinic should be asked to be a member of the work group for the school health services characteristic. Include a parent and student representative on each work group. Additionally, try to include community volunteers with expertise in a given area: it would be advantageous to have a local public health officer, pediatrician, or pediatric nurse practitioner serve on the school health services characteristic work group.

To help you keep track of your progress, each section in this action tool includes tools that will help you to identify and record

- Tasks that you need to complete under each activity.
- Unanticipated actions that you need to undertake.
- Individuals responsible for completion of each activity.
- Targeted completion dates for every activity.
- Evidence to document that you've completed each activity.

A quick review of the Healthy School Report Card may lead you to consider scoring the characteristics sequentially over a long time frame rather than setting up simultaneous scoring processes. Pilot schools found that they experienced greater success with school improvement planning when all work groups worked simultaneously to score the entire Healthy School Report Card, because some of the information gathered for one characteristic may help you respond to indicators in another characteristic. In addition, the process outlined in the action tool is as important to your successful engagement of community members as the data you collect.

Each school has its own rhythm within the school year. Plan the timing of your work so that scoring the Healthy School Report Card does not place any additional time burdens on the school staff. Schools that have been using the Healthy School Report Card were most successful in getting staff support when scoring did not coincide with the standardized test

Step 1

Step 1

period. Some schools organized their work groups and gathered documents during the summer. Select the time of year that works best in your community, keeping in mind your goal of creating a healthy school with the support of your community.

Once your school has fully scored the Healthy School Report Card, you can enter the information in the Healthy School Communities online analysis tool. The purchase of this manual entitles your school to unlimited access to the results analysis tool found on ASCD's Healthy School Report Card website at www.healthyschoolcommunities.org/reportcard. On the website, you will be able to establish your own password and enter the data. The tool will then generate a scoring summary that provides a color-coded planning priority rating.

Your steering committee should determine how to coordinate the data entry for the Healthy School Report Card. Base your decision on the resources that are available in your school. Some teams that have used the Healthy School Report Card had one person enter the data for all of the sections; other schools assigned one individual per work group to the data-entry role. In both situations, the steering committee should take responsibility for coordinating the data entry.

RESOURCES

American Association for Health Education. (n.d.). *National health education standards: For students.* Retrieved from http://www.gdoe.net/ci/hlth_ed_supp/Nat_Hlth_Ed_Std.pdf

Association of State and Territorial Health Officials. (n.d.). [Home page]. Retrieved from www.astho.org

Canadian Association for Health, Physical Education, Recreation and Dance. (2009). [Home page]. Retrieved from www.cahperd.ca

Communities and Schools Promoting Health. (n.d.). *School health policies.* Retrieved from www.safehealthyschools.org/shpolicies/school_health_policies.htm

National Association of State Boards of Education. (n.d.). *Weblinks to state education agencies.* Retrieved from www.nasbe.org/SEA_Links/SEA_Links.html

Smith, J. (2003). *Education and public health: Natural partners in learning for life.* Alexandria, VA: ASCD.

Taras, H., Duncan, P., Luckenbill, D., Robinson, J., Wheeler, L., & Wooley, S. (2004). *Health, mental health and safety guidelines for schools.* Retrieved from www.nationalguidelines.org

U.S. Department of Education. (n.d.). *Education resource organizations directory.* Retrieved from http://wdcrobcolp01.ed.gov/Programs/EROD/org_list_by_territory.cfm

ASCD © 2010. All Rights Reserved.

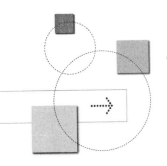

Tools for Organizing

Getting Ready for the Healthy School Report Card

Use these tools as you lay the groundwork for support.

Objective: Receive approval for scoring the Healthy School Report Card from the appropriate school district or school officials who have the appropriate level of authority.			
Activity	**Person Responsible**	**Completion Date**	**Evidence of Completion**

ASCD © 2010. All Rights Reserved.

Tools for Organizing

Step 1

Objective: Complete a marketing and awareness campaign to generate support for completing the Healthy School Report Card and recruit stakeholder participants.			
Activity	**Person Responsible**	**Completion Date**	**Evidence of Completion**

ASCD © 2010. All Rights Reserved.

Tools for Organizing

Objective:
Implement strategies for managing administrator and participant expectations about data collection and planning in lieu of extensive, immediate programmatic change.

Activity	Person Responsible	Completion Date	Evidence of Completion

Step 1

ASCD © 2010. All Rights Reserved.

Objective:
Determine the Healthy School Report Card completion pattern—entire school district, school clusters, or individual schools.

Activity	Person Responsible	Completion Date	Evidence of Completion

ASCD © 2010. All Rights Reserved.

Objective:
Acquire and organize the support and resources needed to collect and interpret Healthy School Report Card data.

Activity	Person Responsible	Completion Date	Evidence of Completion

ASCD © 2010. All Rights Reserved.

Establishing a Steering Committee

Use these tools as you establish a steering committee.

Objective: Prepare and approve a committee charge, which includes a statement of purpose and expectations.			
Activity	**Person Responsible**	**Completion Date**	**Evidence of Completion**

ASCD © 2010. All Rights Reserved.

Tools for Organizing

Objective:
Draft an agenda including the date, time, and place for an initial organizing meeting.

Activity	Person Responsible	Completion Date	Evidence of Completion

Step 1

ASCD © 2010. All Rights Reserved.

Step 1

Objective: Select and invite potential members to attend an initial meeting.			
Activity	**Person Responsible**	**Completion Date**	**Evidence of Completion**

ASCD © 2010. All Rights Reserved.

Tools for Organizing

Objective:
Prepare for the initial meeting.

Activity	Person Responsible	Completion Date	Evidence of Completion

Step 1

ASCD © 2010. All Rights Reserved.

Step 1

Objective: Hold the initial meeting.			
Activity	**Person Responsible**	**Completion Date**	**Evidence of Completion**

ASCD © 2010. All Rights Reserved.

Tools for Organizing

Objective:
Conduct follow-up activities, including contacting meeting attendees.

Activity	Person Responsible	Completion Date	Evidence of Completion

ASCD © 2010. All Rights Reserved.

Sample Steering Committee Charge

Review this sample charge and write an appropriate one for your committee.

A charge serves to keep a group's work on track. The steering committee's charge should reflect its overarching responsibility for completion of the process, from inception to final report. Each work group will have a specific charge that includes the assessment, data input, and use of the data analysis to make recommendations to the full steering committee.

Below is a sample charge to a school health steering committee.

Health and safety issues can serve as barriers to learning and teaching. In addition, a school in which some students, staff, or community members do not feel safe, secure, and supported is itself less than conducive to learning. These issues can be managed in a school through a coordinated approach that ensures compliance with comprehensive policies that are designed to address positive health and academic outcomes for students and staff.

This steering committee will use the Healthy School Report Card to conduct an assessment to determine our school's strengths and shortcomings to assist us in becoming a high-quality, health-promoting school. The steering committee will establish a time line for completion of the assessment and will form work groups, and members will serve as work group chairs to coordinate the assessment process. This committee will draft a summary report of findings and make recommendations for actions to be included in the school improvement plan.

ASCD © 2010. All Rights Reserved.

Community Partners

Use this tool as you consider who to invite to be on the steering committee.

Membership on a healthy school steering committee and on the work groups should be as representative of the entire school community as possible. Identify the key players in your community. Involve people with a broad variety of education, experience, opinion, economic level, gender, race, age, and ethnic background. Some of the community members listed may serve well as steering committee members while others would be important on a work group assessing a specific set of services.

Community Members (Name, Affiliation)	Invited	Accepted	Attended
Attorneys:			
_____	☐	☐	☐
_____	☐	☐	☐
Business and industry leaders:			
_____	☐	☐	☐
_____	☐	☐	☐
Civic, service, and professional organization representatives:			
_____	☐	☐	☐
_____	☐	☐	☐
Clergy:			
_____	☐	☐	☐
_____	☐	☐	☐
Clients and customers of community services:			
_____	☐	☐	☐
_____	☐	☐	☐
Community leaders:			
_____	☐	☐	☐
_____	☐	☐	☐
Community government officials:			
_____	☐	☐	☐
_____	☐	☐	☐
Extension specialists:			
_____	☐	☐	☐
_____	☐	☐	☐

Step 1

Step 1

Community Members (Name, Affiliation)	Invited	Accepted	Attended
Health care providers:			
Clinic _____	☐	☐	☐
Dental _____	☐	☐	☐
Dietitian _____	☐	☐	☐
Emergency _____	☐	☐	☐
Hospital _____	☐	☐	☐
Medical services _____	☐	☐	☐
Mental health _____	☐	☐	☐
Human service agencies:			
Child protection services _____	☐	☐	☐
Drug and alcohol			
counseling _____	☐	☐	☐
Public health _____	☐	☐	☐
Juvenile court system:			
Judge _____	☐	☐	☐
Probation officer_____	☐	☐	☐
Nonprofit service providers:			
_____	☐	☐	☐
_____	☐	☐	☐
Parents:			
_____	☐	☐	☐
_____	☐	☐	☐
_____	☐	☐	☐
_____	☐	☐	☐
_____	☐	☐	☐
Parent–teacher organization representatives:			
_____	☐	☐	☐
_____	☐	☐	☐
_____	☐	☐	☐
Police department officials:			
_____	☐	☐	☐
_____	☐	☐	☐
_____	☐	☐	☐

ASCD © 2010. All Rights Reserved.

Community Members (Name, Affiliation)	Invited	Accepted	Attended
Public media members:			
_____	☐	☐	☐
_____	☐	☐	☐
_____	☐	☐	☐
School personnel:			
Area education agency representative _____	☐	☐	☐
Coach _____	☐	☐	☐
Counselor _____	☐	☐	☐
Family and Consumer Science teacher _____	☐	☐	☐
Food service worker _____	☐	☐	☐
Health teacher _____	☐	☐	☐
In-school support services provider _____	☐	☐	☐
Physical education teacher _____	☐	☐	☐
Principal _____	☐	☐	☐
Special education teacher _____	☐	☐	☐
School board member _____	☐	☐	☐
School social worker _____	☐	☐	☐
School nurse _____	☐	☐	☐
Teacher _____	☐	☐	☐
Students:			
_____	☐	☐	☐
_____	☐	☐	☐
Student government representative _____	☐	☐	☐
Volunteer health agency representatives:			
_____	☐	☐	☐
_____	☐	☐	☐
_____	☐	☐	☐

Step 1

Step 1

Community Members (Name, Affiliation)	Invited	Accepted	Attended
Youth groups members:			
_____	☐	☐	☐
_____	☐	☐	☐
_____	☐	☐	☐
Senior citizens:			
_____	☐	☐	☐
_____	☐	☐	☐
_____	☐	☐	☐
Others:			
_____	☐	☐	☐
_____	☐	☐	☐
_____	☐	☐	☐
_____	☐	☐	☐

Source: Adapted from *Healthy Schools—Healthy Kids* by the Texas American Cancer Society. Retrieved October 10, 2005, from www.schoolhealth.info. Copyright 2004 by Texas American Cancer Society. Reprinted with permission.

ASCD © 2010. All Rights Reserved.

Sample Invitation to Participate Letter

Use this sample letter for your first steering committee meeting. Print your letter on school letterhead.

[Date]

[Title, Name, Position]

[Address]

[City, State, Zip]

Dear [Title, Name]:

Our schools' administration recognizes the importance of creating a school that supports the well-being of our students and staff to improve their abilities to learn and teach. To begin this work, we will assess our current efforts to create a healthy environment for our students and staff and compare those results with best practices recognized on the local, state, and national levels.

Our first step is to develop a steering committee that includes key members of our school and community. We invite you to be a member of this committee. The work we do together will identify our strengths and our services already in place, as well as illuminate areas for improvement. Ultimately, our work will identify priorities, describe activities, and develop time lines that will result in a school culture that supports a coordinated approach to meeting the health, safety, and academic needs of our students.

Our organizational meeting will be held [date, time, and location]. Please contact _____ by phone_____ or e-mail _____ by_____ [date] to express your interest in joining this effort.

Your participation will help us create a high-quality school that supports positive outcomes for our students and our community.

We look forward to seeing you at the meeting.

Sincerely,
[superintendent]   [school leader]

Step 1

Sample Invitation Response Form

Use this tool with the invitation letter. This could be printed on a self-addressed, stamped postcard.

_____ YES, I would like to serve on the Healthy School Steering Committee and will attend the organizational meeting.

_____ YES, I'm interested in serving as a member of the Healthy School Steering Committee, but I cannot attend the meeting. Please keep me on your list and inform me of future plans.

_____ NO, I'm not interested in being involved at this time. Please remove my name from your list.

Name: _____

Position: _____

Address: _____

City: _____ State: _____ ZIP: _____

Work phone: _____ Home phone: _____ Fax: _____

E-mail address: _____

Source: Adapted from *Healthy Schools—Healthy Kids* by the Texas American Cancer Society. Retrieved October 10, 2005, from www.schoolhealth.info. Copyright 2004 by the Texas American Cancer Society. Reprinted with permission.

ASCD © 2010. All Rights Reserved.

Sample Agenda for the Organizational Meeting

Use this sample agenda tool for your first meeting.

Healthy School Steering Committee Meeting
[Date, Time, Location]

Objectives:

    To gain commitment for creating a healthy school

    To outline the process for assessing the school's health environment

    To establish a steering committee

Get Acquainted (15 minutes)

- Refreshments
- Sign-in
- Name tags

Welcome (5 minutes, school leader in charge of facilitating this initiative)

- Introduce yourself
- Thank those attending for their interest
- Introduce the superintendent

Opening Remarks (10 minutes, superintendent or principal)

- Describe a health-promoting school and the administration's commitment to this project.
- Clarify the potential envisioned and the results hoped for with the creation of this steering committee and use of the Healthy School Report Card.
- Express appreciation for everyone's attendance, interest, and commitment to helping improve the school community.
- Ask attendees for their support to the process.

Introductions (10 minutes, leader in charge of facilitating this inititiative)

- Ask those attending to introduce themselves, identify their affiliation, and explain what motivated them to attend.

Overview of Steering Committee (15 minutes, meeting chair)

- Provide an overview of the process.
- Discuss the membership of the steering committee.
- Describe the role of the steering committee and the expectations for the members.
- Explain the role of the work groups in the assessment process.

Feedback and Question-and-Answer Period (15 minutes)

- Open up discussion to all members.

Next Steps (15 minutes)

- Set the next meeting date, time, and location.
  - ○ Indicate the next steps that need to be taken and ask for agreement on those steps as the purpose for the next meeting.
    - ▪ Complete a thorough review of the Healthy School Report Card.
    - ▪ Determine a time line and process, and form multiple work groups.
- Ask for volunteers to help plan and lead the next meeting. Set a planning time with those volunteers to prepare for the next steering committee meeting.
- Ask for the names, addresses, phone numbers, and e-mail addresses of others who should be invited to the next meeting.
- Remind the volunteers that their active involvement is important.

Adjournment (5 minutes, superintendent or principal)

- Thank participants again for their attendance and input.

ASCD © 2010. All Rights Reserved.

Forming Multiple Work Groups

Copy these tools for all groups to complete as needed for tracking work group formation and progress.

Objective:
Appoint chairs of multiple work groups and prepare them to facilitate Healthy School Report Card scoring.

Activity	Person Responsible	Completion Date	Evidence of Completion

Step 1

Objective:
Work with chairs to recruit appropriate, qualified, and interested work group members.

Activity	Person Responsible	Completion Date	Evidence of Completion

ASCD © 2010. All Rights Reserved.

Tools for Organizing

Objective:
Distribute documents containing a charge to each work group with a list of tasks and proposed time line.

Activity	Person Responsible	Completion Date	Evidence of Completion

Step 1

ASCD © 2010. All Rights Reserved.

Step 1

Objective:
Establish the processes within each group for compiling scores and data input.

Activity	Person Responsible	Completion Date	Evidence of Completion

ASCD © 2010. All Rights Reserved.

Tools for Organizing

Objective: Determine who within each group will be responsible for completing a draft report.			
Activity	**Person Responsible**	**Completion Date**	**Evidence of Completion**

Step 1

ASCD © 2010. All Rights Reserved.

Resources

Association of State and Territorial Health Officials. (n.d.). ASTHO [Home page]. Retrieved from http://www.astho.org

Canadian Association for Health, Physical Education, Recreation and Dance. (2005). CAH-PERD [Home page]. Retrieved from http://www.cahperd.ca/

Communities and Schools Promoting Health. (n.d.). *School health policies.* Retrieved from http://www.safehealthyschools.org/shpolicies/school_health_policies.htm

Egerter, S., Braveman, P., Sadegh-Nobari, T., Grossman-Kahn, R., & Dekker, M. (2009, September). Education matters for health. *Issue Brief, 6.* Retrieved from http://www.rwjf .org/files/research/commission2009eduhealth.pdf

National Association of State Boards of Education. (n.d.). *State school healthy policy database.* Retrieved from http://nasbe.org/healthy_schools/hs/index.php

National Center for Chronic Disease Prevention and Health Promotion. (2007). *CDC's school health education resources (SHER): National health education standards (NHES).* Retrieved from http://www.cdc.gov/healthyyouth/sher/standards/

Smith, J. (2003). *Education and public health: Natural partners in learning for life.* Alexandria, VA: ASCD.

Taras, H., Duncan, P., Luckenbill, D., Robinson, J., Wheeler, L., & Wooley, S. (2004). *Health, mental health and safety guidelines for schools.* Retrieved from www.national guidelines.org

U.S. Department of Education. (n.d.). *Education resource organizations directory.* Available: http://wdcrobcolp01.ed.gov/Programs/EROD/org_list_by_territory.cfm

ASCD © 2010. All Rights Reserved.

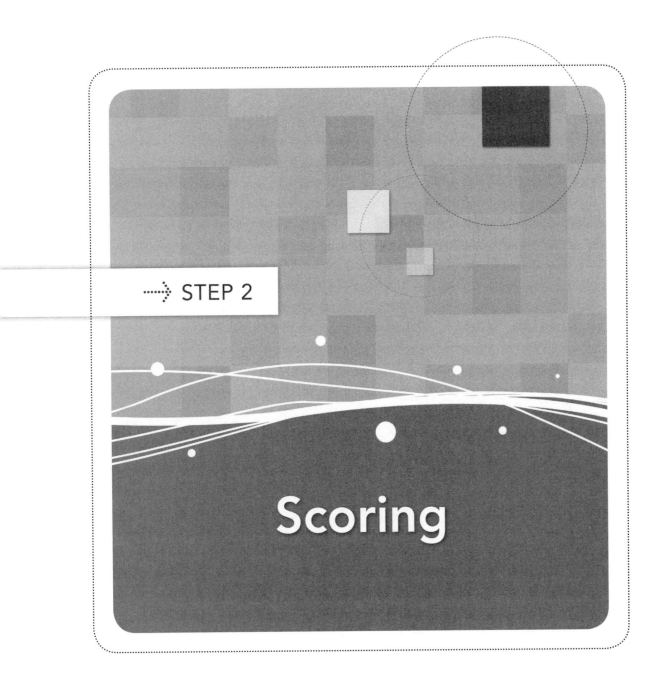

STEP 2

Scoring

Scoring Your School

The Healthy School Report Card is structured around health-promoting school characteristics, with indicators that describe aspects of a health-promoting school. The characteristics directly relate to all the components of a coordinated school health program plus overall coordination, policy, and strategic planning. The characteristics and indicators are purposely limited to a select number of statements that describe the structural factors within the school that need to be present for each component to exist and function at a high level of quality, for health programming to be coordinated, and for Healthy School Communities to become institutionalized within the school. (Descriptions of these characteristics are presented later.)

Now that you have completed the preliminary work and identified the work group membership, each work group can begin the assessment using the Healthy School Report Card by

- Outlining the orientation and scoring tasks for each work group.
- Using the tools included in this section to gather background information that will assist with completion of the report card.
- Completing the electronic spreadsheet to record input.

DEVELOPING A COMMON UNDERSTANDING

Before attempting to score the Healthy School Report Card, work group members need to know and have a common understanding of the indicators under their assigned characteristic. Some indicators are straightforward, so accomplishing this won't take much time or effort. For example, the food and nutrition services characteristic (8) work group could easily reach a common understanding of indicator 1d: A high-quality, nutritional breakfast is available for students every day. On the other hand, the school facilities and transportation characteristic (5) work group would probably need to devote considerable energy to determining and understanding all the standards that are encompassed within indicator 1c:

Environmental quality standards are met (i.e., water, temperature, lighting, sewage, ventilation, indoor air quality, sound, sanitation, pest control, hazardous materials, and blood-borne pathogen and exposure control). The point is that each work group should devote the time and effort needed to fully comprehend each indicator before attempting to complete its segment of the report card.

Each work group should determine standards for scoring the indicators and should consult resources that can provide guidance for scoring the indicators as needed. For example, to score Characteristic 8's indicator 1d, the work group will have to establish a standard for a high-quality, nutritional breakfast. If the person in charge of your school lunch program and a dietitian from the community are on the work team, they can provide guidance. Documents, books, instruments, and websites can also be valuable resources. You may need to contact your state's or province's education department, health department, or other agencies to acquire guidance specific to your locale. Websites that can help you are listed on page 58 and throughout this action tool.

Work group members should also have a common understanding of the questions and ratings they will be using to score each indicator. For example, Question 1 for each indicator asks, "To what extent does the standard set by this indicator appear in my school?" Response options are (1) does not exist, (2) partially met, (3) fully met, or (4) exceeds. To give meaning to these response options, scores need to remain consistent. Work groups should think of the response options like this:

1. **Does not exist:** Our school doesn't do this at all; we don't have anything in place.
2. **Partially met:** Our school does this to some extent; however, either some aspect of the indicator is missing or what we have does not fully meet the standard described by the indicator.
3. **Fully met:** Our school does this in a way that fully meets both the standards of scope and quality described by the indicator.
4. **Exceeds:** Our school does this in a way that clearly surpasses both the standards of scope and quality described by the indicator.

For instance, work groups would score indicator 1b of Characteristic 3: Social and Emotional Climate (Students are taught and expected to practice sound coping, anger management, negotiation, and communication skills.) in this way:

ASCD © 2010. All Rights Reserved.

- A score of 1 would be given if students in the school are neither taught these skills nor expected to practice them in school. The indicator just does not exist.
- A score of 2 would be given if students in the school are taught these skills in health class but are not clearly expected to employ these skills in school. The indicator is only partially met because the skills are taught but the expectation of use is missing.
- A score of 3 would be given if students in the school are taught these skills in health class and the health teacher or other teachers or administrators express clear, overt, and repeated expectations. Signs or other information signaling that these skills are employed on a regular basis in school are evident in the school. The indicator is met.
- A score of 4 would be given if all the conditions in the score of 3 are met and a school-wide, thematic unit on collaboration is offered, accompanied by a dramatic reduction in disciplinary referrals for arguing, fighting, or other such behaviors. Clear evidence exists that your school has gone beyond the letter of the indicator to truly exceed the standard expressed in it.

After scoring each assigned indicator for Question 1, work groups should review their assigned indicators two more times to provide scores for Question 2 and Question 3.

For Question 2, "How much will a change in this indicator improve the health and safety of students and staff?," work groups will give each indicator one of four possible ratings: (1) very little, (2) some, (3) quite a bit, or (4) a lot.

1. **Very little:** Very little change would result if this indicator were improved.
2. **Some:** Some change would result if this indicator were improved.
3. **Quite a bit:** Quite a bit of change would result if this indicator were improved.
4. **A lot:** A lot of change would result if this indicator were improved.

Question 3, "How much effort will it take to significantly change the current status of this indicator?," can have one of four possible ratings: (1) very little, (2) some, (3) a lot, or (4) overwhelming.

1. **Very little:** Very little effort would be needed to produce a significant change.
2. **Some:** Some effort would be needed to produce a significant change.
3. **A lot:** A lot of effort would be needed to produce a significant change.
4. **Overwhelming:** Overwhelming effort would be needed to produce a significant change.

GATHERING INFORMATION

To fully clarify the meaning of each characteristic and indicator for their school, work group members should gather the necessary background information. Before they can begin scoring, work groups should review all the indicators under the characteristics they are responsible for and determine if they have sufficient information to accurately answer Question 1. One way to expedite this process, which many schools have found helpful, is to distribute copies of the characteristics and indicators—either electronically or as a hard copy—to work group members before an initial scoring meeting so that they can become familiar with the indicators they will asked to score and bring to the meeting any background information that may be helpful for informing others.

If work groups are satisfied that they have sufficient information, they can begin scoring. Some work groups, however, may find that they do not know enough about the status of one or more of the indicators they are responsible for. This may hold true for many of the indicators for Characteristic 5: School Facilities and Transportation. Likewise, some work groups may feel that they should gather input from a wider representation of the school to be able to rate an indicator definitively. This may hold true for many indicators for Characteristic 3: Social and Emotional School Climate. Whatever the case, work groups should gather more information when they believe they cannot make a sound, informed judgment with the information at hand. Using the "Preliminary Assessment of Question 1" tool on page 75 will help you determine how well your team can answer Question 1 and, if needed, who will gather the information.

Information gathering can take many forms. It may be as simple as reviewing existing documents or as complex as surveying large constituencies such as faculty members, parents, and students. You may consider the following information-gathering strategies.

- **Document review:** Members of the work group access and review school or school district documents that contain the needed information.
- **Oral reports:** School or school district staff members with specialized knowledge provide information through a presentation to the work group.
- **Interviews:** Work group members identify individuals who have the needed information and meet with them to get answers to prepared questions.
- **Focus groups:** Work group members convene one or more small groups of individuals representing specific school constituencies and ask them to respond orally to questions prepared by the work group.

 © 2010. All Rights Reserved.

Step 2

- **Surveys:** Work group members ask specific constituencies to provide responses to a prepared survey that is administered either on paper or electronically.

When choosing a strategy, work groups should select the one that will yield the desired information with the least amount of burden to themselves and others. For instance, information gathered from well-selected focus groups may be just as useful as survey data collected from much larger groups. Additionally, work groups may need assistance with more sophisticated strategies, such as focus groups or surveys. For example, student and parent surveys and focus groups are most conducive to the following indicators:

- Characteristic 3: Social and Emotional Climate indicators 1c, 3b, 3c, 3d, 5a, 5b, and 5c
- Characteristic 4: Family and Community Involvement indicators 1a and 1b
- Characteristic 8: Food and Nutrition Services indicators 1a, 1b, 3f, and 3g

Rather than asking work groups to score the entire Healthy School Report Card, some schools have opted to administer their report card as a survey, in much the same way traditional school improvement surveys have been administered. If you take this approach, you would distribute the Healthy School Report Card to a broad cross section of school stakeholders, including staff members, students, and parents. However, you should be aware of a couple of caveats:

- Although scores from stakeholder groups can be useful for a variety of reasons, data from those groups may reflect more their perceptions or customer satisfaction rather than fact. For example, when asked to complete the Healthy School Report Card anonymously, parents and students in one school rated indicator 3a of Characteristic 3: Social and Emotional Climate (A student code of conduct and discipline clearly delineates behaviors that lead to suspension, expulsion, or other sanctions, including possession or use of weapons, tobacco products, alcohol and other drugs, violence, bullying, and harassment.) as "does not exist," whereas school administrators completing the report card during a meeting rated this indicator as "fully met." Both groups reported accurately based on their own knowledge. The administrators know that a student code of conduct exists, but, because it is not distributed or reviewed on a regular basis, most students and parents were not aware of its existence. Therefore, uncovering both the facts and perceptions about the code of conduct is important.
- Some stakeholder groups may not have access to the information needed to score a number of the Healthy School Report Card indicators and may feel frustrated if asked

ASCD © 2010. All Rights Reserved.

to do so. To be scored properly, some indicators require specialized, expert knowledge that only school staff possess, but the majority of the indicators can be scored by parents, students, and other stakeholders. Nonexperts serving on work groups can score indicators accurately once members establish a common understanding of the scoring process as well as what each indicator pertains to.

If you administer the Healthy School Report Card to a broader audience of stakeholders, such as students and parents, communication is paramount. You should address two key issues ahead of time:

- Stakeholders are not expected to be able to score all indicators, and, rather than feel frustrated, they should skip any indicators they do not feel qualified to score.
- Stakeholders' perceptions or opinions are valued, even if the stakeholders do not have access to complete factual information about some indicators.

To assure accuracy and quality, use of work groups is still highly recommended, even if you take a survey approach to the Healthy School Report Card. Work groups should be formed around each characteristic to gather factual information and interpret scores from a wider group of stakeholders. Members of each work group should be assigned specific indicators and be aware of the time line. Each group should schedule a time to meet to review the assessment of each indicator and to discuss the outcomes for its portion of the Healthy School Report Card. A single copy of the report card should be submitted to the person designated to complete the data entry (see page 30 for suggestions about how to designate data entry responsibilities).

After gathering information, all work groups should go through their assigned indicators to score Question 1, Question 2, and Question 3. Accurate, informed scores for these questions are crucial for establishing the priorities your school will include in its Healthy School Improvement Plan. Once it has scored all indicators, the work group should submit its completed Healthy School Report Card segments to the person or people designated to do data entry.

INTERPRETING AND INPUTTING THE DATA

The methods you choose for collecting data for the Healthy School Report Card will affect your results. When analyzing the data, you may notice that sometimes ratings generated from many participants seem at odds with ratings generated by school experts. If this occurs,

ASCD © 2010. All Rights Reserved.

you'll need to find out why the difference exists. Sometimes the school experts are privy to more complete information or may have a more positive view of their area of responsibility than survey respondents. Both the experts and the survey respondents may be correct, but because they are viewing the indicator from different vantage points, they may have different perceptions.

This was the case in two schools that used surveys to gather information. In both schools, many survey participants—students, staff, and parents—rated indicators such as Characteristic 8: Food and Nutrition Services indicator 1a (Meals offered in the cafeteria meet U.S. Department of Agriculture nutritional guidelines.) and indicator 1c (The cafeteria offers to students and staff foods that are low in fat, salt, and sugar.) as "does not exist" or "partially met." In contrast, the school food service staff rated both as being "fully met."

It turned out that the food service staff members could show that they had gone to great lengths to change the nutritional quality of the food they served. However, because they had not informed any of their customers of the changes, they did not get recognition for their efforts. The school experts were rating indicators based on facts, and others were rating them on perceptions. Data can't always tell the whole story. Where discrepancies appear, go beyond the data by asking additional questions.

When you are ready to enter your Healthy School Report Card data into the online analysis tool, go to www.healthyschoolcommunities.org/reportcard, log in, and follow the on-screen instructions.

Once you've submitted your data for evaluation, the tool will then generate a scoring summary that provides a color-coded planning priority rating. You will need Adobe Acrobat Reader to open the files, which you can print.

ASCD © 2010. All Rights Reserved.

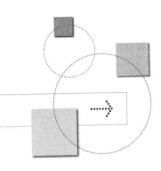

Tools for Scoring

Step 2

ASCD © 2010. All Rights Reserved.

Reviewing and Clarifying Characteristics and Indicators

Copy and complete these tools for each work group.

Objective: Prior to each work group meeting, distribute the appropriate section of the Healthy School Report Card to each work group for review.			
Activity	**Person Responsible**	**Completion Date**	**Evidence of Completion**

Objective:
Within each work group, develop a consistent common, understanding of the characteristics and indicators through review and discussion.

Activity	Person Responsible	Completion Date	Evidence of Completion

ASCD © 2010. All Rights Reserved.

Step 2

Standards for Scoring Indicators

Copy and complete these tools for each work group.

Objective: Analyze characteristics and indicators to determine the appropriate level of assessment (i.e., school district or school).			
Activity	**Person Responsible**	**Completion Date**	**Evidence of Completion**

Step 2

 © 2010. All Rights Reserved.

Step 2

Objective: Gather documentation and background information from appropriate documents, internal experts, external experts, and other sources and share with all work group members.			
Activity	**Person Responsible**	**Completion Date**	**Evidence of Completion**

ASCD © 2010. All Rights Reserved.

Preliminary Assessment of Question 1

Copy and complete these tools for each work group.

Objective: Review all indicators to determine if available information is sufficient to allow for scoring.			
Activity	**Person Responsible**	**Completion Date**	**Evidence of Completion**

ASCD © 2010. All Rights Reserved.

Step 2

	Objective:
	Gather and distribute to work group members additional documentation and background information from appropriate documents, internal experts, external experts, and other sources.

Activity	Person Responsible	Completion Date	Evidence of Completion

ASCD © 2010. All Rights Reserved.

The Healthy School Report Card
Progress Report

Use these tools to outline the steering committee's tasks.

Objective:
Through facilitated work group meetings, determine and enter appropriate scores for each of the three questions (i.e., existence, benefit, effort), being sure to cover every indicator.

Activity	Person Responsible	Completion Date	Evidence of Completion

Step 2

Step 2

Objective: Gather indicator scores from every work group, making sure that all characteristics and indicators are addressed.			
Activity	**Person Responsible**	**Completion Date**	**Evidence of Completion**

ASCD © 2010. All Rights Reserved.

Objective:
Enter indicator scores for every characteristic in the online analysis tool at www.healthyschool communities.org/reportcard and print the generated color-coded output document.

Activity	Person Responsible	Completion Date	Evidence of Completion

Step 2

ASCD © 2010. All Rights Reserved.

The Healthy School Report Card

You are now ready to begin scoring your school with the Healthy School Report Card. If you don't already have one in place, the steering committee could become your school's health or wellness team. Your district's school health council and school's health team should assume special responsibility for setting and accomplishing objectives for characteristics 1 and 2.

Characteristics 1 and 2 provide the umbrella for all other school health activities. They address implementation and institutionalization of essential structures (i.e., policy, health coordinator, school health team, and school health council) as well as policy compliance, data collection, and strategic planning, which are critical for a health-promoting school. Most schools have some programs that fit under characteristics 3–11; however, these programs are seldom coordinated, resulting in gaps and overlaps that hinder the best use of limited resources.

If you have an established school health team and a fully functioning, coordinated approach to school health, assessing characteristics 1 and 2 will give you the opportunity to showcase the important work the team is doing to institutionalize the indicators across your school.

If you are establishing a school health team or improving an existing team, characteristics 1 and 2 provide the basis for using best practices and guidelines at the outset. Scoring the indicators will help you prioritize your strategic planning, policy, and coordinating activities.

Characteristic 1: School Health Program Policy and Strategic Planning

A school health system should ultimately be judged by results—improved student behavior and staff and student health status that lead to the reduction or elimination of barriers to learning and teaching. A high-quality approach cannot produce results unless it is well established, coordinated, supported, and institutionalized over time. Schools are governed by formal policies, usually adopted by a board of education, which establish priorities and specify actions school staff must take to comply.

For a school to institutionalize a coordinated approach, it must have a portfolio of policies that covers multiple aspects of each characteristic of a healthy school, as well as overall coordination. Policy examples are available at www.ascd.org/healthyschoolcommunities. Note that the wellness policy mandated under the Child Nutrition and WIC Reauthorization Act, though important to many aspects of coordinated school health, is only one of many health-related policies that school districts must or are well-advised to adopt. The policy indicators listed under Characteristic 1 refer to the broad collection of health-related policies and not solely to the mandated wellness policy.

To be in a position to comply with these policies, school staff members, including administrators and supervisors, must be aware of policies and have the requisite preparation and resources to implement them. In addition, you must monitor and, if inadequate, improve policy compliance. At established intervals, you should prepare and renew plans based on student health status data and health and safety program data.

Your state or provincial departments of education and health may have staff designated to assisting localities in establishing a coordinated approach to school health. These experts can also provide technical assistance and guidance on meeting the requirements your governing body has developed.

SCORING TIPS

⋯⟩ You may choose to assign this characteristic to the steering committee, particularly if your school is just beginning coordination efforts.

⋯⟩ This work group should include a school administrator.

ASCD © 2010. All Rights Reserved.

The Healthy School Report Card

CHARACTERISTIC 1: SCHOOL HEALTH PROGRAM POLICY AND STRATEGIC PLANNING

Description: My school maintains a culture that supports health through compliance with comprehensive policies that address all aspects of a coordinated approach to school health.	Question 1 To what extent does the standard set by this indicator appear in your school? 1 - Does not exist 2 - Partially met 3 - Fully met 4 - Exceeds	Question 2 How much will a change in this indicator improve the health and safety of students and staff? 1 - Very little 2 - Some 3 - Quite a bit 4 - A lot	Question 3 How much effort will it take to significantly change the current status of this indicator? 1 - Very little 2 - Some 3 - A lot 4 - Overwhelming
1. Policy, Professional Development, Monitoring, and Compliance			
a. The health program is governed by an extensive set of school board-approved policies that are consistent with best practice recommendations of state and federal agencies or professional education and health organizations.			
b. All health program staff members, including health education and physical education teachers, are properly credentialed and well qualified.			
c. All staff members responsible for health program policy implementation participate in regularly scheduled professional development activities.			
d. All staff members are provided the time and resources required to comply with health program policies.			
e. Administrators and supervisors attend professional development that prepares them to authoritatively monitor health policy compliance.			
f. Administrators and supervisors routinely monitor health policy compliance and take action to remedy deficiencies.			
2. Strategic Planning and Evaluation			
a. Strategic plans are periodically developed for all aspects of the health program, including coordination.			
b. The Healthy School Improvement Plan is the basis for the annual school improvement plan.			

Step 2

ASCD © 2010. All Rights Reserved.

83

Step 2

CHARACTERISTIC 1: SCHOOL HEALTH PROGRAM POLICY AND STRATEGIC PLANNING *(continued)*

Description: My school maintains a culture that supports health through compliance with comprehensive policies that address all aspects of a coordinated approach to school health.	Question 1 To what extent does the standard set by this indicator appear in your school? 1 - Does not exist 2 - Partially met 3 - Fully met 4 - Exceeds	Question 2 How much will a change in this indicator improve the health and safety of students and staff? 1 - Very little 2 - Some 3 - Quite a bit 4 - A lot	Question 3 How much effort will it take to significantly change the current status of this indicator? 1 - Very little 2 - Some 3 - A lot 4 - Overwhelming
2. Strategic Planning and Evaluation *(continued)*			
c. Confidential student health indicator data are collected at least once every two years and are carefully considered when determining strategic plan objectives and activities.			
d. Results of periodic health program needs and status assessments are carefully considered in the strategic planning process.			
e. Progress toward fully implementing the health program strategic plan is monitored on a regular basis.			
f. Benefits of the school health program to participants (e.g., better health), the school (e.g., improved attendance), and the school district (e.g., reduced costs) are identified and reported.			

RESOURCES

The following resources will help you maintain a supportive culture through comprehensive policies that address all aspects of a coordinated school health program.

Allensworth, D., Lawson, E., Nicholson, L., & Wyche, J. (Eds.). (1997). *Schools and health: Our nation's investment.* Washington, DC: National Academy Press.

Bogden, J. F. (2000). *Fit, healthy, and ready to learn: A school health policy guide—Parts I and II.* Alexandria, VA: National Association of State Boards of Education.

Council of Chief State School Officers and the Association of State and Territorial Health Officials. (2003). *The school health starter kit* (2nd ed.). Washington, DC: Council of Chief State School Officers.

Greene, B. Z., & McCoy, K. I. (1998). The national role in coordinated school health programs. In E. Marx, S. F. Wooley, & D. Northrop (Eds.), *Health is academic: A guide to coordinated school health programs* (pp. 269–291). New York: Teachers College Press.

ASCD © 2010. All Rights Reserved.

Levi, J., Vinter, S., Richardson, L., St. Laurent, R., & Segal, L. M. (2009). *F as in fat 2009: How obesity policies are failing America*. Retrieved from http://healthyamericans.org/reports/obesity2009/Obesity 2009Report.pdf

Lohrmann, D. K. (2006). Process evaluation for school health professionals. *Journal of School Health,76*(4), 154–155.

National Center for Chronic Disease Prevention and Health Promotion. (2010). *Nutrition, physical activity, and childhood obesity: Local wellness policy tools and resources*. Retrieved from http://www.cdc.gov/ HealthyYouth/healthtopics/wellness.htm

National Center for Chronic Disease Prevention and Health Promotion. (2010). *Student health and academic achievement*. Retrieved from http://www.cdc.gov/HealthyYouth/health_and_academics/index .htm

National School Boards Association. (2010). *Search the school health database* [Database]. Available from http://www.nsba.org/MainMenu/SchoolHealth/SearchSchoolHealth.aspx

Robert Wood Johnson Foundation. (2009, June). *RWJF research brief—Local school wellness policies: How are schools implementing the congressional mandate?* Retrieved from http://www.rwjf.org/files/ research/20090708localwellness.pdf

Sweeney, D. B., & Nichols P. (1998). The state role in coordinated school health programs. In E. Marx, S. F. Wooley, & D. Northrop (Eds.), *Health is academic: A guide to coordinated school health programs* (pp. 244–268). New York: Teachers College Press.

U.S. Department of Agriculture Food and Nutrition Service. (n.d.) *Local wellness policy*. Retrieved from http://www.fns.usda.gov/tn/Healthy/wellnesspolicy.html

RECOMMENDED ASCD RESOURCES

ASCD. (2007). *The learning compact redefined: A call to action*. Retrieved from http://www.wholechild education.org/resources/Learningcompact7-07.pdf

Grebow, P. M., Greene, B. Z., Harvey, J., & Head, C. J. (2000). Shaping health policies. *Educational Leadership, 57*(6), 63–66.

Johnson, D. P. (2005). *Sustaining change in schools: How to overcome differences and focus on quality*. Alexandria, VA: ASCD.

Lambert, L. (2003). *Leadership capacity for lasting school improvement*. Alexandria, VA: ASCD.

Lewallen, T. C. (2004, August). Healthy learning environments. *ASCD InfoBrief, 38.*

Marx, E., & Checkley, K. (2003). *An ASCD professional development online course: Supporting student health and achievement*. Alexandria, VA: ASCD.

Osorio, J., Marx, E., & Bauer, L. (2000). Finding the funds for health resources. *Educational Leadership, 57*(6), 30–32.

Smith, J. (2003). *Education and public health: Natural partners in learning for life*. Alexandria, VA: ASCD.

Westbrook, J., & Spiser-Alberb, V. (2002). *Creating the capacity for change: An ASCD action tool*. Alexandria, VA: ASCD.

Step 2

ASCD © 2010. All Rights Reserved. 85

Characteristic 2: Coordination of School Health Programs

Many school health programs evaluate each characteristic or component separately without looking at the quality of the coordination of their efforts. Coordination is a key element in creating a healthy school. The effort your school puts into implementing essential organizational structures and conducting effective coordination strategies will pay off in a number of ways: Intentional and strategic coordination reduces competition among staff for access to resources, and it eliminates gaps and overlaps in programs and services. Coordination will help ensure that your combined staff will deal proactively with the health and safety issues of any student or staff member.

SCORING TIP

----> You may choose to have the steering committee assigned to score this characteristic, particularly if your school is just beginning coordination efforts. The information you gather through the Healthy School Report Card will provide guidance on moving those efforts forward.

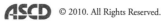

© 2010. All Rights Reserved.

Step 2

CHARACTERISTIC 2: COORDINATION OF SCHOOL HEALTH PROGRAMS

Description: The culture in my school facilitates coordination of all health programs to eliminate gaps and overlaps, expand access to health resources, and ensure high quality.	**Question 1** To what extent does the standard set by this indicator appear in your school? **1** - Does not exist **2** - Partially met **3** - Fully met **4** - Exceeds	**Question 2** How much will a change in this indicator improve the health and safety of students and staff? **1** - Very little **2** - Some **3** - Quite a bit **4** - A lot	**Question 3** How much effort will it take to significantly change the current status of this indicator? **1** - Very little **2** - Some **3** - A lot **4** - Overwhelming
1. Essential Structures			
a. School staff members responsible for health program components meet regularly as a school health team to coordinate activities.			
b. A school health council or coalition made up of the school health team, a parent or guardian, and community and business representatives functions effectively.			
c. Persons with substantial influence in the school or community (e.g., physicians, dentists, medical administrators, parents, civic or business leaders, school board members, high-level school administrators) are strong advocates for school health.			
d. A designated staff member (e.g., administrator, nurse, teacher, counselor) is responsible for ensuring coordination of health programs.			
e. A designated staff member is responsible for ensuring compliance with the Child Nutrition and WIC Reauthorization Act wellness policy mandate, especially the implementation, monitoring, and evaluation requirements.			
f. Sufficient resources (e.g., funds, staff time, space) are provided to support the health program.			
2. Essential Activities			
a. When a new health problem arises, school staff members from different health programs routinely coordinate plans and activities aimed at alleviating the problem.			

Step 2

 © 2010. All Rights Reserved.

☐ 87

CHARACTERISTIC 2: COORDINATION OF SCHOOL HEALTH PROGRAMS *(continued)*

Description: The culture in my school facilitates coordination of all health programs to eliminate gaps and overlaps, expand access to health resources, and ensure high quality.	**Question 1** To what extent does the standard set by this indicator appear in your school? **1** - Does not exist **2** - Partially met **3** - Fully met **4** - Exceeds	**Question 2** How much will a change in this indicator improve the health and safety of students and staff? **1** - Very little **2** - Some **3** - Quite a bit **4** - A lot	**Question 3** How much effort will it take to significantly change the current status of this indicator? **1** - Very little **2** - Some **3** - A lot **4** - Overwhelming
2. Essential Activities *(continued)*			
b. School staff members responsible for health programs blend resources (e.g., funding, materials, staff time) from different sources.			
c. School health staff members regularly inform the principal, district superintendent, or school board of current developments in the school health program.			
d. School health staff members communicate with key constituencies (e.g., school staff, parents or guardians, community members, business and industry representatives) at least monthly.			

RESOURCES

The following resources will help you eliminate gaps and overlaps, expand access to health programming, and ensure high quality.

Allensworth, D., Lawson, E., Nicholson, L., & Wyche, J. (Eds.). (1997). *Schools and health: Our nation's investment.* Washington, DC: National Academy Press.

Butterfoss, F. D., & Kegler, M. C. (2002). Toward a comprehensive understanding of community coalitions: Moving from practice to theory. In R. J. DiClemente, R. A. Crosby, & M. C. Kegler (Eds.), *Emerging theories in health promotion practice and research* (pp. 157–191). San Francisco, CA: Jossey-Bass.

Center for Health and Health Care in Schools. (2007). [Home page]. Retrieved from http://www.healthinschools.org

Fetro, J. V. (1998). Implementing coordinated school health programs in local schools. In E. Marx, S. F. Wooley, & D. Northrop (Eds.), *Health is academic: A guide to coordinated school health programs* (pp. 15–42). New York: Teachers College Press.

Fetro, J. V. (1998). *Step by step to health promoting schools.* Santa Cruz, CA: ETR Associates.

ASCD © 2010. All Rights Reserved.

Step 2

Health, Mental Health and Safety Guidelines for Schools. (n.d.) *Overarching guidelines*. Retrieved from http://www.nationalguidelines.org/chapter_full.cfm?chapter=overarching

Johnson, A. J., & Breckon, D. J. (2007). *Managing health education and promotion programs: Leadership skills for the 21st century*. Boston: Jones and Bartlett Publishers.

Lohrmann, D. K. (2008). A complimentary ecological model of coordinated school health promotion. *Public Health Reports, 123*(6), 695–703.

McKenzie, F. D., & Richmond, J. B. (1998). Linking health and learning: An overview of coordinated school health programs. In E. Marx, S. F. Wooley, & D. Northrop (Eds.), *Health is academic: A guide to coordinated school health programs* (pp. 1–14). New York: Teachers College Press.

National Center for Chronic Disease Prevention and Health Promotion. (2010). *School health policy*. Retrieved from http://www.cdc.gov/HealthyYouth/policy/index.htm

Rogers, E. M. (2003). *Diffusion of innovations* (5th ed.). New York: The Free Press.

Wiley, D. C., & Howard-Barr, E. M. (2005). Advocacy to action: Addressing coordinated school health program issues with school boards. *Journal of School Health, 75*, 6–9.

Wilkinson, M. (2004). *The secrets of facilitation: The S.M.A.R.T. guide to getting results with groups*. San Francisco, CA: Jossey-Bass.

RECOMMENDED ASCD RESOURCES

ASCD. (2009). *L2L webinar series: Creating a healthy school community*. Available from https://admin.na4.acrobat.com/_a824650571/p65505378/

Brown, J. L. (2004). *Making school improvement happen with what works in schools: School-level factors: An ASCD action tool*. Alexandria, VA: ASCD.

Lewallen, T. C. (2004, August). Healthy learning environments. *ASCD InfoBrief, 38*.

Reeves, D. B. (2009). *Leading change in your school: How to conquer myths, build commitment, and get results*. Alexandria, VA: ASCD.

Zmuda, A., Kuklis, R., & Kline E. (2004). *Transforming schools: Creating a culture of continuous improvement*. Alexandria, VA: ASCD.

Step 2

ASCD © 2010. All Rights Reserved. 89

Step 2

HS RC Characteristic 3: Social and Emotional Climate

The social and emotional climate in a school and in the classroom affects students' abilities to learn and to feel connected to their teachers and school. Students who feel connected to school are more likely to have improved attitudes toward school, learning, and teachers; higher academic goals and achievements; and fewer risk behaviors (Blum, 2005), especially related to alcohol, tobacco, and other drug use as well as sexual activity and intentional violence. At the school level, indicators of positive social and emotional climates include student and family ownership, student bonding, and student conduct and discipline. At the classroom level, indicators involve instructional practice, classroom tone, student self-management, and classroom management.

These proven practices are associated with less disruptive student behavior, more time on task, and higher academic achievement. They also contribute to healthy relationships, the development of staff-student-school connectedness, and positive health behaviors. Research has shown that effective teachers of all school subjects implement these types of practices in their classrooms.

SCORING TIPS

····} The work group scoring this characteristic may wish to interview students and staff or administer student and staff surveys for some of the indicators.

····} A school administrator may use classroom observations to score the classroom climate indicators.

ASCD © 2010. All Rights Reserved.

CHARACTERISTIC 3: SOCIAL AND EMOTIONAL CLIMATE

Description: The culture in my school is conducive to making students, families, and staff members feel safe, secure, accepted, and valued.	Question 1 To what extent does the standard set by this indicator appear in your school? 1 - Does not exist 2 - Partially met 3 - Fully met 4 - Exceeds	Question 2 How much will a change in this indicator improve the health and safety of students and staff? 1 - Very little 2 - Some 3 - Quite a bit 4 - A lot	Question 3 How much effort will it take to significantly change the current status of this indicator? 1 - Very little 2 - Some 3 - A lot 4 - Overwhelming
1. Overall School Climate: Expectations for Students and Staff			
a. Through oral presentations and print materials, students are informed of what they must do to be responsible, successful, contributing members of a learning community.			
b. Students are taught and expected to practice sound coping, anger management, negotiation, and communication skills.			
c. Staff members display the same levels of civility and respect to each other and to students as students are expected to display toward each other and adults.			
2. Overall School Climate: Ownership and Bonding			
a. Students, school staff, and parents or guardians participate in establishing school norms and rules.			
b. Students function in smaller groupings or within smaller school structures such as schools within the school.			
c. Structured programs assist students with transitions (e.g., middle to high school, new to the school) through which they also learn the norms and culture of the school.			
d. A wide array of extracurricular activities is available to students.			
e. Before-school and after-school latchkey programs are available to students.			
f. Both structured and informal academic and nonacademic opportunities to collaborate with others are available to students.			

Step 2

Step 2

CHARACTERISTIC 3: SOCIAL AND EMOTIONAL CLIMATE *(continued)*

Description: The culture in my school is conducive to making students, families, and staff members feel safe, secure, accepted, and valued.	**Question 1** To what extent does the standard set by this indicator appear in your school? 1 - Does not exist 2 - Partially met 3 - Fully met 4 - Exceeds	**Question 2** How much will a change in this indicator improve the health and safety of students and staff? 1 - Very little 2 - Some 3 - Quite a bit 4 - A lot	**Question 3** How much effort will it take to significantly change the current status of this indicator? 1 - Very little 2 - Some 3 - A lot 4 - Overwhelming
2. Overall School Climate: Ownership and Bonding *(continued)*			
g. Students have opportunities to engage the school and community through service learning and other sponsored programs.			
3. Overall School Climate: Conduct and Discipline			
a. The school clearly articulates how it expects students and staff to conduct themselves and behave and outlines steps for ensuring that all school participants comply.			
b. Rules of conduct are fairly, consistently, and uniformly enforced for all students.			
c. Disciplinary penalties are appropriate and constructive.			
d. School rules apply equally to school staff members and students.			
4. Within Individual Classrooms: Opportunity to Learn			
a. Teachers provide a robust curriculum based on their thorough knowledge of the subject and the methods that are most effective for teaching it.			
b. Teachers identify essential content and provide all students ample opportunity to learn it.			
5. Within Individual Classrooms: Classroom Tone			
a. Teachers emphasize and model mutual respect for all persons in their classrooms.			

 © 2010. All Rights Reserved.

CHARACTERISTIC 3: SOCIAL AND EMOTIONAL CLIMATE *(continued)*

Description: The culture in my school is conducive to making students, families, and staff members feel safe, secure, accepted, and valued.	**Question 1** To what extent does the standard set by this indicator appear in your school? **1** - Does not exist **2** - Partially met **3** - Fully met **4** - Exceeds	**Question 2** How much will a change in this indicator improve the health and safety of students and staff? **1** - Very little **2** - Some **3** - Quite a bit **4** - A lot	**Question 3** How much effort will it take to significantly change the current status of this indicator? **1** - Very little **2** - Some **3** - A lot **4** - Overwhelming
5. Within Individual Classrooms: Classroom Tone *(continued)*			
b. Teachers support and have high expectations for all students.			
c. Teachers treat all students fairly, consistently, and uniformly.			
6. Within Individual Classrooms: Classroom Student Self-Management			
a. Teachers promote students' use of learned cooperative skills including listening carefully, disagreeing respectfully, and compromising.			
b. Teachers expect students to assume age-appropriate responsibility for learning through effective decision making, goal setting, and time management.			
7. Within Individual Classrooms: Classroom Management			
a. Teachers apply clear routines, rules, and behavioral expectations, which students participate in establishing and maintaining.			
b. Teachers arrange seating and traffic patterns to facilitate learning and classroom management.			
c. Teachers reinforce prosocial behavior.			
d. Teachers assess misbehavior to determine the cause and the purpose* the misbehavior serves for the student.			
e. Teachers select interventions based on an understanding of the cause and purpose* of the misbehavior.			

*The purpose of misbehavior may be idiosyncratic to the cultural or socioeconomic status of a student and may be inconsistent with the traditional middle class behavioral expectations found in most schools.

 © 2010. All Rights Reserved.

RESOURCES

The following resources will help you develop a safe, healthy, and supportive school climate.

Adelman, H. (1998). School counseling, psychological, and social services. In E. Marx, S. F. Wooley, & D. Northrop (Eds.), *Health is academic: A guide to coordinated school health programs* (pp. 142–168). New York: Teachers College Press.

Benard, B. (n.d.). *Resilience: What we have learned.* San Francisco: WestEd.

Freiberg, H. J. (1999). *School climate: Measuring, improving and sustaining healthy learning environments.* Philadelphia, PA: Falmer Press.

Gilman, R., Huebner, E. S., & Furlong, M. J. (2009). *Handbook of positive psychology in schools.* New York: Routledge.

Hanson, T. L., Austin, G., & Lee-Bayha, J. (2004). *Ensuring that no child is left behind: How are student health risks and resilience related to the academic progress of schools?* Retrieved from http://www.wested .org/online_pubs/hd-04-02.pdf

Health, Mental Health and Safety Guidelines for Schools. (n.d.) *Social environment.* Retrieved from http:// www.nationalguidelines.org/chapter_full.cfm?chapter=social

Knoff, H. M. (2001). *The stop and think social skills program teacher's manual: Grades preK–8.* Boston, MA: Sopris West. Available from http://www.projectachieve.info/productsandresources/thestopthinksocial skillsprogramschool.html

Los Angeles County Office of Education. (2000). *Classroom management: A California resource guide.* (Available from Los Angeles County Office of Education, Safe Schools Center, 9300 Imperial Highway, Downey, CA 90242-2890)

Quality counts 2008: Tapping into teaching, unlocking the key to student success. (2008). *Education Week, 27*(18). Retrieved from http://www.edweek.org/ew/toc/2008/01/10/index.html

U.S. Department of Education. (n.d.). *Doing what works: Dropout prevention* [Home page]. Retrieved from http://dww.ed.gov/topic/?T_ID=24

RECOMMENDED ASCD RESOURCES

Blum, R. W. (2005). A case for school connectedness. *Educational Leadership, 62*(7), 16–20.

Bosher, W., Kaminski, K. R., & Vacca, R. S. (2004). *The school law handbook: What every leader needs to know.* Alexandria, VA: ASCD.

Creating caring schools. (2003). *Educational Leadership, 60*(6).

Cummings, C. (2000). *Winning strategies for classroom management.* Alexandria, VA: ASCD.

Engaging the whole child. (2007). *Educational Leadership, 64*(9). Retrieved from http://www.ascd.org/ publications/educational-leadership/summer07/vol64/num09/toc.aspx

Erwin, J. C. (2004). *The classroom of choice: Giving students what they need and getting what you want.* Alexandria, VA: ASCD.

Learning First Alliance. (2001). *Every child learning: Safe and supportive schools.* Alexandria, VA: ASCD.

McCloskey, M. (2007). The whole child. *ASCD Infobrief, 51.* Retrieved from http://www.ascd.org/ publications/newsletters/infobrief/fall07/num51/toc.aspx

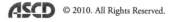
© 2010. All Rights Reserved.

McLeod, J., Fisher, J., & Hoover, G. (2003). *The key elements of classroom management: Managing time and space, student behavior, and instructional strategies.* Alexandria, VA: ASCD.

Novick, B., Kress, J. S., & Elias, M. J. (2002). *Building learning communities with character: How to integrate academic, social, and emotional learning.* Alexandria, VA: ASCD.

Scherer, M. (Ed.). (2010). *Keeping the whole child healthy and safe: Reflections on best practices in learning, teaching, and leadership.* Alexandria, VA: ASCD. Available from http://shop.ascd.org/productdisplay.cfm?productid=110130E4

Shaps, E. (2003). Creating a school community: Building a strong sense of community in schools is both important and doable. *Educational Leadership, 60*(6), 31–33.

Strong, J. H. (2002). *Qualities of effective teachers.* Alexandria, VA: ASCD.

Step 2

Characteristic 4: Family and Community Involvement

Successful student outcomes depend heavily on students' family involvement in their education. Family members and the broader community can contribute to the success of school health programming by providing resources and expertise in school, educating students outside school hours, reinforcing healthy behaviors through role modeling, and creating a community environment that supports positive behaviors. Family involvement in school health programming also benefits the community when family members receive health information from the school. School facilities that are open to the community generally find greater community engagement and approval for support and resources.

The Healthy School Report Card integrates family and community involvement indicators, as appropriate, into individual characteristics that you will score. Family and community involvement is so integral to the broader healthy school context that it has a separate characteristic for you to assess.

SCORING TIP

⋯⋯⟩ If you hold focus groups or conduct surveys to gather information for the family involvement indicator, consider including questions that can help the work groups for other characteristics gather information related to family involvement. For example, a survey or focus group process will supply data to use with Characteristic 6: Health Education if you include questions about the health education materials that are sent home and data for Characteristic 8: Food and Nutrition Services if you include questions about nutrition and food safety materials.

ASCD © 2010. All Rights Reserved.

CHARACTERISTIC 4: FAMILY AND COMMUNITY INVOLVEMENT

Description: The culture in my school encourages, supports, and facilitates involvement of parents or guardians and the broader community in health programming.	**Question 1** To what extent does the standard set by this indicator appear in your school? **1** - Does not exist **2** - Partially met **3** - Fully met **4** - Exceeds	**Question 2** How much will a change in this indicator improve the health and safety of students and staff? **1** - Very little **2** - Some **3** - Quite a bit **4** - A lot	**Question 3** How much effort will it take to significantly change the current status of this indicator? **1** - Very little **2** - Some **3** - A lot **4** - Overwhelming
1. Family Involvement			
a. Families are welcomed by all staff as partners in the education of their children.			
b. Family members are encouraged to visit the school.			
c. The school has a family resource room that includes information about health resources.			
d. School outreach workers offer school orientation and social and health services to families via home visits.			
e. Health-related parent education programs are conducted.			
f. Families are provided information about health-related education programs offered in the community.			
g. Family members serve on school health committees.			
h. School health staff members routinely collaborate with parent groups (e.g., PTA or PTO, Safe Homes).			
2. Community Involvement			
a. Community members participate in mentoring programs for at-risk youth.			
b. School health programs are routinely coordinated with local health department programs for children, adolescents, and families.			
c. The school health program is included in overall community health planning.			

Step 2

CHARACTERISTIC 4: FAMILY AND COMMUNITY INVOLVEMENT *(continued)*

Description: The culture in my school encourages, supports, and facilitates involvement of parents or guardians and the broader community in health programming.	**Question 1** To what extent does the standard set by this indicator appear in your school? 1 - Does not exist 2 - Partially met 3 - Fully met 4 - Exceeds	**Question 2** How much will a change in this indicator improve the health and safety of students and staff? 1 - Very little 2 - Some 3 - Quite a bit 4 - A lot	**Question 3** How much effort will it take to significantly change the current status of this indicator? 1 - Very little 2 - Some 3 - A lot 4 - Overwhelming
2. Community Involvement *(continued)*			
d. Public health and social service agencies provide services to families after regular school hours.			
e. Public health department, public safety agency, community social service agency, and medical and dental facility staff members participate on health committees, provide consultation and training, and serve as guest speakers.			
f. Outside agencies (e.g., public health, public safety, hospitals, businesses, foundations) secure funding and other resources for school health and safety programs.			
g. Public health, public safety, social service, medical, and dental agencies provide services to students during the school day.			
h. Outside regular school hours, school facilities are used to provide personal development, educational, health, social, and recreational programming for the community.			

RESOURCES

The following resources will help you encourage, support, and facilitate involvement of parents or guardians and the broader community.

Carlyon, P., Carlyon, W., & McCarthy, A. R. (1998). Family and community involvement in school health. In E. Marx, S. F. Wooley, & D. Northrop (Eds.), *Health is academic: A guide to coordinated school health programs* (pp. 67–95). New York: Teachers College Press.

Center for the Education and Study of Diverse Populations at New Mexico Highlands University. (2007). *Working together: School-family-community partnerships* [Home page]. Retrieved from http://www.cesdp.nmhu.edu/toolkit/index.html

ASCD © 2010. All Rights Reserved.

Dryfoos, J. G. (1994). *Full service schools: A revolution in health and social services for children, youth, and families.* San Francisco: Jossey-Bass.

Health, Mental Health and Safety Guidelines for Schools. (n.d.). *Family and community involvement.* Retrieved from http://www.nationalguidelines.org/chapter_full.cfm?chapter=family

Institute of Medicine. (2009). *Local government actions to prevent childhood obesity.* Washington, DC: National Academies Press.

National Association of State Boards of Education. (2009). *Partners in prevention: The role of school-community partnerships in dropout prevention.* Retrieved from http://www.nasbe.org/index.php/file-repository/func-startdown/1007/

RECOMMENDED ASCD RESOURCES

Allen, R. (2005). New paradigms for parental involvement: Stronger family role in schools seen as key to achievement. *Education Update, 47*(3), 3–5.

ASCD. (2009). *L2L webinar series: Developing successful community partnerships.* Retrieved from http://ascd.na4.acrobat.com/p91523757/

Blank, M., & Berg, M. (2006, July). *All together now: Sharing responsibility for the whole child.* Retrieved from http://www.ascd.org/ASCD/pdf/sharingresponsibility.pdf

Building schools that build learners. (2006). *Education Update, 48*(11). Retrieved from http://www.ascd.org/publications/newsletters/education-update/nov06/vol48/num11/toc.aspx

Tapping parent and community support to improve student learning. (2008). *Education Update, 50*(4). Retrieved from http://www.ascd.org/publications/newsletters/education-update/apr08/vol50/num04/toc.aspx

Step 2

Characteristic 5: School Facilities and Transportation

The school physical environment can promote safety and community in ways that support learning and teaching. Students and staff who feel safe and work together in facilities that are well kept can focus on their daily tasks. Their sense of security will be enhanced by emergency plans that are reviewed periodically and that include coordination with community resources.

On the other hand, poor lighting, inadequate ventilation, and environmental toxins in schools have a negative impact on student and staff wellness—affecting attendance, concentration, and learning. As one principal said, "If my students don't feel physically safe in my school, I've already lost in my efforts to foster a positive learning environment."

School leaders should be especially interested in this characteristic because conditions such as overcrowding; poor lighting; inadequate ventilation; uncomfortable air temperature; persistent, excessive noise; and environmental toxins, including secondhand smoke, mold, mildew and chemical fumes, are all stressors that have demonstrable negative effects on student and staff health and well-being. Furthermore, compliance with many of the school facilities and transportation indicators is required by various federal and state laws and has been positively linked to reduction in risk-management and liability costs.

SCORING TIP

⤑ This characteristic cuts across a number of areas for which district-level staff may have the expertise you need to score the indicators. Separate work groups could be assigned to score this characteristic, with one assigned to safety and quality (indicators 1a–1i) and one assigned to security and emergencies (indicators 2a–2f and 3a–3b). If you use separate work groups, they should meet to make sure that all members can discuss their recommendations for the report to the steering committee.

ASCD © 2010. All Rights Reserved.

CHARACTERISTIC 5: SCHOOL FACILITIES AND TRANSPORTATION

Description: The culture in my school ensures that buildings, grounds, and vehicles are secure and meet all established safety and environmental standards.	**Question 1** To what extent does the standard set by this indicator appear in your school? **1** - Does not exist **2** - Partially met **3** - Fully met **4** - Exceeds	**Question 2** How much will a change in this indicator improve the health and safety of students and staff? **1** - Very little **2** - Some **3** - Quite a bit **4** - A lot	**Question 3** How much effort will it take to significantly change the current status of this indicator? **1** - Very little **2** - Some **3** - A lot **4** - Overwhelming
1. Safety and Quality			
a. In collaboration with appropriate state and local agencies, a school committee periodically monitors the safety, security, and environmental quality of buildings, grounds, and school-owned vehicles.			
b. Facilities meet and, preferably, exceed all workplace and public facilities, fire and safety codes, rules, and regulations.			
c. Environmental quality standards are met (i.e., water, temperature, lighting, sewage, ventilation, indoor air quality, sound, sanitation, pest control, hazardous materials, and blood-borne pathogen and exposure control).			
d. Facilities are structurally sound and free of defects.			
e. Facilities, grounds, and vehicles are alcohol, drug, tobacco, and smoke free.			
f. Allergens that can trigger asthma and food allergy attacks are minimized to the greatest possible extent.			
g. Facilities and grounds have structural features and plantings that limit sun exposure.			
h. The bus fleet is maintained in accordance with state safety and operating standards.			
i. Through a formal reporting, tracking, and investigation system, causes of injuries to students and staff are determined and, if possible, eliminated.			

Step 2

CHARACTERISTIC 5: SCHOOL FACILITIES AND TRANSPORTATION *(continued)*

Description: The culture in my school ensures that buildings, grounds, and vehicles are secure and meet all established safety and environmental standards.	**Question 1** To what extent does the standard set by this indicator appear in your school? **1 -** Does not exist **2 -** Partially met **3 -** Fully met **4 -** Exceeds	**Question 2** How much will a change in this indicator improve the health and safety of students and staff? **1 -** Very little **2 -** Some **3 -** Quite a bit **4 -** A lot	**Question 3** How much effort will it take to significantly change the current status of this indicator? **1 -** Very little **2 -** Some **3 -** A lot **4 -** Overwhelming
2. Security			
a. Effective natural surveillance structures (e.g., clear lines of sight, no isolated areas) are present and, as needed, augmented by electronic surveillance devices.			
b. All school entrances are monitored to deny access to intruders.			
c. Visitors must register in the main office and wear a pass at all times.			
d. Smooth traffic flow is facilitated by wide halls and stairs, no bottlenecks, and limited and controlled access.			
e. The number of well-qualified security staff is adequate to meet the school's needs.			
f. Internal common areas and external grounds and play areas are supervised by adults before and after school, during recess, and at lunchtime.			
3. Emergencies			
a. Emergencies (e.g., weather, violence, bioterrorism) are handled through planned procedures in accordance with recommendations of state and national emergency management and criminal justice agencies.			
b. Aspects of emergency management strategies are closely coordinated with local law enforcement, emergency response, and medical and mental health agencies and personnel.			

ASCD © 2010. All Rights Reserved.

Step 2

RESOURCES

The following resources will help you meet all established security, safety, and environmental standards for buildings, grounds, and vehicles.

Collaborative for High Performance Schools. (2001). *High performance schools best practices manual.* Available from http://www.chps.net/dev/Drupal/node/288

Frumkin, H., Geller, R. J., & Rubin, I. L. (Eds.). (2006). *Safe and healthy school environments.* New York: Oxford University Press.

Health, Mental Health and Safety Guidelines for Schools. (n.d.). *Physical environment and transportation.* Retrieved from http://www.nationalguidelines.org/chapter_full.cfm?chapter=physical

Healthy Schools Network. (n.d.). *Healthy schools network, inc.* [Home page]. Retrieved from http://www.healthyschools.org

Kerns, J. T., & Ellis, R. E. (2003). *Health and safety guide for K–12 schools in Washington.* Retrieved from http://www.k12.wa.us/SchFacilities/Publications/pubdocs/CompleteSafety&HealthManual2002-2003.pdf

Los Angeles Unified School District, Office of Environmental Health and Safety. (n.d.). *Model safe school plan: A template for ensuring a safe, healthy and productive learning environment.* Retrieved from http://www.lausd-oehs.org/schoolsafetyplans_v1.asp

U. S. Environmental Protection Agency. (2010). *Healthy school environments resources.* Retrieved from http://cfpub.epa.gov/schools/index.cfm

RECOMMENDED ASCD RESOURCES

Healthy bodies, minds, and buildings. (2000). *Educational Leadership, 57*(6).

Learning First Alliance. (2001). *Every child learning: Safe and supportive schools.* Alexandria, VA: ASCD.

Schonfeld, D. J., Lichtenstein, R., Pruett, M. K., & Speese-Linehan, D. (2002). *How to prepare for and respond to a crisis* (2nd ed.). Alexandria, VA: ASCD.

Step 2

Characteristic 6: Health Education

The World Health Organization defines the goals of health education as increasing awareness and favorably influencing attitudes and knowledge relating to the improvement of health on a personal or community basis (World Health Organization, n.d.). Health education should be offered as a documented, planned, and sequential curriculum provided for students each year they are in school (ibid.). The curriculum should be skills-based and provide students with the information they need to be healthy, productive, engaged citizens throughout the course of their lives (ibid.). In the United States, the National Health Education Standards offers a framework that supports the development of health-literate, well-educated citizens through curriculum development, instruction, and assessment (Joint Committee on National Education Standards, 1995).

Family involvement in health education provides a twofold benefit—the health education curriculum can be reinforced at home, and the family members not in school may receive information they would not otherwise have access to.

SCORING TIPS

····⟩ Some indicators differentiate health education methodologies for elementary and middle and high schools. Score those based on your school level. The remainder of the indicators reflect guidelines for all school levels.

····⟩ Your state or province may mandate a different number of hours of health education than the indicators list. Use whichever standard is higher—you are striving to have a high-quality healthy school.

ASCD © 2010. All Rights Reserved.

The Healthy School Report Card

CHARACTERISTIC 6: HEALTH EDUCATION

Description: The culture in my school strongly supports and reinforces the health literacy knowledge, attitudes, behaviors, and skills students learn through a high-quality curriculum.	Question 1 To what extent does the standard set by this indicator appear in your school? 1 - Does not exist 2 - Partially met 3 - Fully met 4 - Exceeds	Question 2 How much will a change in this indicator improve the health and safety of students and staff? 1 - Very little 2 - Some 3 - Quite a bit 4 - A lot	Question 3 How much effort will it take to significantly change the current status of this indicator? 1 - Very little 2 - Some 3 - A lot 4 - Overwhelming
1. Curriculum and Instruction			
a. The health curriculum addresses age-appropriate and developmentally appropriate critical health topics, including social and emotional learning and the six priority health behaviors identified by the Centers for Disease Control and Prevention (CDC),* in a manner that is consistent with state health education standards and frameworks or the National Health Education Standards.			
b. All health curriculum topical units and modules are research-based or consistent with recognized best practice criteria.			
c. Instruction is devoted to mastery of both essential health knowledge and skills (i.e., interpersonal communication, refusal, negotiation, decision making, goal setting, anger management, stress management, safety, first aid, and advocacy).			
d. Student-centered, active teaching strategies are extensively used.			
e. Multiple types of authentic assessment strategies are extensively employed.			
2. Structural Supports			
a. Specific, planned strategies are routinely implemented to support and reinforce healthy behaviors taught through the health curriculum (e.g., the overall school culture supports and reinforces healthy eating choices taught in health education).			

*The six priority child and adolescent health risk behaviors identified by the Centers for Disease Control and Prevention are: intentional and unintentional injury; unhealthy eating; sedentary living; behavior that leads to HIV, STD infection, and unintended pregnancy; tobacco use; and use of alcohol and other drugs.

© 2010. All Rights Reserved.

CHARACTERISTIC 6: HEALTH EDUCATION *(continued)*

Description: The culture in my school strongly supports and reinforces the health literacy knowledge, attitudes, behaviors, and skills students learn through a high-quality curriculum.	**Question 1** To what extent does the standard set by this indicator appear in your school? **1** - Does not exist **2** - Partially met **3** - Fully met **4** - Exceeds	**Question 2** How much will a change in this indicator improve the health and safety of students and staff? **1** - Very little **2** - Some **3** - Quite a bit **4** - A lot	**Question 3** How much effort will it take to significantly change the current status of this indicator? **1** - Very little **2** - Some **3** - A lot **4** - Overwhelming
2. Structural Supports *(continued)*			
b. An advisory committee of administrators, teachers, parents or guardians, students, and community representatives is involved in health curriculum review and revision.			
c. Students in every grade receive at least the recommended minimum 50 hours of health instruction annually.			
d. Health is taught at every grade through specific courses (if a middle or junior high or high school) or by all classroom teachers (if an elementary school).			
e. Students receive regular report card grades in health that are factored into their grade point average.			
f. Health education items are included in elementary, middle, and high school-wide assessments of student achievement.			
3. Family Engagement			
a. Programs are held annually to ensure family awareness of and participation in the more sensitive aspects of health education (e.g., human sexuality, HIV prevention).			
b. Families receive publications that tell them how they can reinforce health lessons their children learn in school.			
c. Some health education homework is designed to be completed with family members.			

ASCD © 2010. All Rights Reserved.

RESOURCES

The following resources will help you build a culture that supports and reinforces health literacy, knowledge, attitudes, behaviors, and skills.

American Alliance for Health, Physical Education, Recreation and Dance: Joint Committee on National Health Education Standards. (1995). *National health education standards: For students.* Retrieved from http://www.gdoe.net/ci/hlth_ed_supp/Nat_Hlth_Ed_Std.pdf

CCSSO-SCASS Health Education Assessment Project. (2006). *Aligning health and reading with a HEAP of books.* Kent, OH: American School Health Association.

Communities and Schools Promoting Health. (n.d.). *Health lesson plans.* Retrieved from http://www .safehealthyschools.org/lessonplansintro.htm

Health, Mental Health and Safety Guidelines for Schools. (n.d.). *Health and safety education.* Retrieved from http://www.nationalguidelines.org/chapter_full.cfm?chapter=health

Joint Committee on National Health Education Standards. (2007). *National health education standards: Achieving excellence* (2nd ed.). Atlanta, GA: American Cancer Society.

Lohrmann, D. K., & Wooley, S. F. (1998). Comprehensive school health education. In E. Marx, S. F. Wooley, & D. Northrop (Eds.), *Health is academic: A guide to coordinated school health programs* (pp. 43–66). New York: Teachers College Press.

Marx, E., & Northrop, D. (1995). *Educating for health: A guide to implementing a comprehensive approach to school health education.* Newton, MA: Education Development Center.

National Center for Chronic Disease Prevention and Health Promotion. (2008). *CDC's school health education resources (SHER)* [Database]. Available from http://apps.nccd.cdc.gov/sher/

National Center for Chronic Disease Prevention and Health Promotion. (2008). *CDC's school health education resources (SHER): Characteristics of an effective health education curriculum.* Retrieved from http:// www.cdc.gov/HealthyYouth/SHER/characteristics/index.htm

National Center for Chronic Disease Prevention and Health Promotion. (2009). *Health education curriculum analysis tool (HECAT).* Retrieved from http://www.cdc.gov/HealthyYouth/HECAT/index.htm

Rothstein, R., & Jacobson, R. (2006). The goals of education. *Phi Delta Kappan, 88,* 264–272.

RECOMMENDED ASCD RESOURCES

Checkley, K. (2000, Spring). Health education: Emphasizing skills and prevention to form a more health-literate people. *Curriculum Update.*

Health and physical education. (2004, Winter). *Curriculum Technology Quarterly, 14*(2).

Health education and physical education. (2002, Spring). *Curriculum Technology Quarterly, 11*(3).

Holt-Hale, S. A., Ezell, G., & Mitchell, M. (2000). *Health and physical education: A chapter of the curriculum handbook.* Alexandria, VA: ASCD.

Lewallen, T. C. (2004, August). Healthy learning environments. *ASCD InfoBrief, 38.*

Step 2

ASCD © 2010. All Rights Reserved. 107

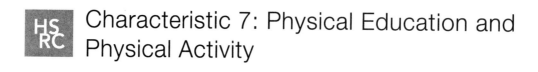

Characteristic 7: Physical Education and Physical Activity

Physical education provides students with skills and education that promote lifelong participation in physical activity and sports through a sequential, developmentally appropriate curriculum. Regular physical activity during childhood and adolescence promotes physical development and prevents or delays the onset of chronic diseases. Research shows a clear and strong link between physical activity and emotional well-being (Centers for Disease Control and Prevention, 2008).

For many students, school is the only place they can engage in safe physical activity. Schools can promote physical activity for their students throughout the school day and for the community by opening their facilities during after-school hours.

SCORING TIPS

----> Consider including the before- and after-school child care program staff on the work group scoring this indicator.

----> Be sure to review how your school provides physical education and activity opportunities for students with disabilities.

----> Some indicators differentiate between elementary and middle and high schools. Score these based on your school level. The balance of the indicators is inclusive of all schools.

----> Your state or province may mandate a different number of physical education hours than noted in the indicator. Use whichever standard is higher—you are striving to have a high-quality healthy school.

ASCD © 2010. All Rights Reserved.

CHARACTERISTIC 7: PHYSICAL EDUCATION AND PHYSICAL ACTIVITY

Description: The culture in my school strongly supports and reinforces the lifelong fitness knowledge, attitudes, behaviors, and skills students learn through a high-quality curriculum.	**Question 1** To what extent does the standard set by this indicator appear in your school? **1** - Does not exist **2** - Partially met **3** - Fully met **4** - Exceeds	**Question 2** How much will a change in this indicator improve the health and safety of students and staff? **1** - Very little **2** - Some **3** - Quite a bit **4** - A lot	**Question 3** How much effort will it take to significantly change the current status of this indicator? **1** - Very little **2** - Some **3** - A lot **4** - Overwhelming
1. Curriculum and Instruction			
a. Physical education emphasizes lifetime physical fitness activities through a curriculum that is consistent with the state's physical education standards or framework or the National Physical Education Standards.			
b. Elementary students receive at least 150 minutes of formal physical education instruction per week; middle or junior high or high school students receive 225 minutes per week.			
c. Students are physically active for at least half of every physical education class session.			
d. Students are taught how to safely engage in all types of physical activity.			
e. Physical education classes have a student–teacher ratio similar to classes in other subjects.			
f. Students are never exempt from taking required physical education because of participation in other activities, such as school sports, marching band, or ROTC.			
g. All students are required to develop and monitor a personal physical activity plan, in addition to participating in physical education.			
2. Structural Supports: Facilities			
a. The teaching area (i.e., gym and outdoor fields) is large enough so that daily physical education can be provided for all students.			

Step 2

CHARACTERISTIC 7: PHYSICAL EDUCATION AND PHYSICAL ACTIVITY *(continued)*

Description: The culture in my school strongly supports and reinforces the lifelong fitness knowledge, attitudes, behaviors, and skills students learn through a high-quality curriculum.	Question 1 To what extent does the standard set by this indicator appear in your school? 1 - Does not exist 2 - Partially met 3 - Fully met 4 - Exceeds	Question 2 How much will a change in this indicator improve the health and safety of students and staff? 1 - Very little 2 - Some 3 - Quite a bit 4 - A lot	Question 3 How much effort will it take to significantly change the current status of this indicator? 1 - Very little 2 - Some 3 - A lot 4 - Overwhelming
2. Structural Supports: Facilities *(continued)*			
b. Physical education facilities are available for teaching throughout the entire school day.			
c. Proper sport and physical activity safety equipment is provided for all students.			
d. The playground has an array of well-designed equipment and structures constructed over safe, soft surfaces.			
3. Structural Supports: Assessment			
a. All students complete an annual physical fitness test and learn how to interpret results.			
b. Individual physical fitness test results are reported to parents or guardians and aggregate results to the community.			
c. Students receive regular report card grades for physical education that are factored into their overall grade point average.			
4. Opportunities for Physical Activity			
a. Semi-structured games and other activities are offered during recess and lunch periods.			
b. Students can participate in a wide array of competitive and noncompetitive physical activity options through school intramurals or physical activity clubs.			
c. Before-school and after-school child care programs include opportunities for participation in a variety of competitive and noncompetitive physical activities.			

ASCD © 2010. All Rights Reserved.

CHARACTERISTIC 7: PHYSICAL EDUCATION AND PHYSICAL ACTIVITY *(continued)*

Description: The culture in my school strongly supports and reinforces the lifelong fitness knowledge, attitudes, behaviors, and skills students learn through a high-quality curriculum.	**Question 1** To what extent does the standard set by this indicator appear in your school? **1 -** Does not exist **2 -** Partially met **3 -** Fully met **4 -** Exceeds	**Question 2** How much will a change in this indicator improve the health and safety of students and staff? **1 -** Very little **2 -** Some **3 -** Quite a bit **4 -** A lot	**Question 3** How much effort will it take to significantly change the current status of this indicator? **1 -** Very little **2 -** Some **3 -** A lot **4 -** Overwhelming
4. Opportunities for Physical Activity *(continued)*			
d. Every effort is made to collaborate with community-based organizations, including use of school play fields, pools, and gyms, to make supervised physical activity opportunities available to students and families after school hours, on weekends, and during breaks, including summers.			
e. Physical activity is not used or withheld as punishment.			

Step 2

RESOURCES

The following resources will help you support and reinforce lifelong fitness knowledge, attitudes, behaviors, and skills through high-quality curriculum.

Annie E. Casey Foundation. (n.d.). *Kids count* [Home page]. Retrieved from http://www.kidscount.org

Centers for Disease Control and Prevention. (1997). Guidelines for school and community programs to promote lifelong physical activity among young people. *Morbidity and Mortality Weekly Report: Recommendations and Reports, 46*(RR-6). Available from http://www.cdc.gov/healthyyouth/physicalactivity/guidelines/index.htm

Centers for Disease Control and Prevention. (2008). *Make a difference at your school*. Retrieved from http://www.cdc.gov/HealthyYouth/keystrategies/pdf/make-a-difference.pdf

Centers for Disease Control and Prevention. (2010). *Division of nutrition, physical activity and obesity* [Home page]. Retrieved from http://www.cdc.gov/nccdphp/dnpa/recommendations.htm

Department of Health and Human Services. (2005). *The president's council on physical fitness and sports* [Home page]. Retrieved from http://www.fitness.gov

Hannaford, C. (2005). *Smart moves: Why learning is not all in your head*. Salt Lake City, UT: Great River Books.

Health, Mental Health and Safety Guidelines for Schools. (n.d.). *Physical education*. Retrieved from http://www.nationalguidelines.org/chapter_full.cfm?chapter=physEd

National Association for Sport and Physical Education. (n.d.). *NASPE national standards*. Retrieved from http://www.aahperd.org/naspe/standards/nationalStandards/index.cfm

National Association for Sport and Physical Education. (2004). *Moving into the future: National standards for physical education* (2nd ed.). Reston, VA: Author.

National Center for Chronic Disease Prevention and Health Promotion. (2008). *Physical education curriculum analysis tool (PECAT)*. Available from http://www.cdc.gov/HealthyYouth/PECAT/index.htm

National Consortium for Physical Education and Recreation for Individuals with Disabilities. (1995). *Adapted physical education national standards (APENS)*. Champaign, IL: Human Kinetics.

National School Boards Association. (2010). *Childhood obesity and schools* [Home page]. Retrieved from http://www.nsba.org/MainMenu/SchoolHealth/obesity-and-schools.aspx

Paterson, K. (2007). *3-minute motivators: More than 100 simple ways to reach, teach and achieve more than you ever imagined*. Markham, Canada: Pembroke Publishers.

Physical and Health Education Canada. (2009). *Quality daily physical education* [Home page]. Retrieved from http://www.cahperd.ca/eng/physicaleducation

Ratey, J. J. (2008). *Spark the revolutionary new science of exercise and the brain*. New York: Little, Brown and Company.

Seefeldt, V. D. (1998). Physical education. In E. Marx, S. F. Wooley, & D. Northrop (Eds.), *Health is academic: A guide to coordinated school health programs* (pp. 116–141). New York: Teachers College Press.

RECOMMENDED ASCD RESOURCES

Franklin, J. (2004, Winter). Shaping up at school: Programs aim to promote fitness and nutrition. *Curriculum Update.*

Health and physical education. (2004, Winter). *Curriculum Technology Quarterly, 14*(2).

Health education and physical education. (2002, Spring). *Curriculum Technology Quarterly, 11*(3).

Holt, S. A., Hale, G. E., & Murray, M. (2002). *Health and physical education: A chapter of the curriculum handbook*. Alexandria, VA: ASCD.

Lambert, L. T. (2000). The new physical education. *Educational Leadership, 57*(6), 34–38.

Step 2

ASCD © 2010. All Rights Reserved.

HS RC Characteristic 8: Food and Nutrition Services

Food and nutrition services play a multifaceted role in the development of students. Food insufficiency in communities is frequently addressed through school nutrition programs. When schools offer students nutritional food that supports their ability to concentrate in school and grow physically, they are also reinforcing the nutrition information students learned in health education to develop healthy eating patterns. The environment in which students eat can help them develop social skills and influences their feelings of safety and control.

Schools can also provide information to staff and families about healthy eating and food safety. Some schools have found that student involvement in growing produce served in school meals, taste-testing new products, and selecting healthy items for vending machines provides benefits in establishing a more engaged student population.

There is a widespread consensus about the role of the school in promoting healthy eating behaviors and providing appropriate access to healthy food options before, during, and after the school day, as well as at school-sponsored events. Furthermore, there's now research evidence on best nutritional practices (Stallings & Yaktine, 2007). Now, school decision makers have clear and explicit guidance about the food and nutrition policies and practices that serve the best interests of students and staff members alike.

The following indicators are based on the standards for foods offered in school that were identified by the Institute of Medicine in 2007.

SCORING TIPS

----> Students can be helpful in scoring this characteristic by conducting surveys and interviews to gather the information for their assigned sections.

----> Data collection methods will affect your results. Staff experts' perceptions of the food and nutrition services may vary from those of students and other staff.

ASCD © 2010. All Rights Reserved.

Step 2

CHARACTERISTIC 8: FOOD AND NUTRITION SERVICES

Description: The culture in my school supports, promotes, and reinforces healthy eating patterns and food safety for students and staff.	Question 1 To what extent does the standard set by this indicator appear in your school? 1 - Does not exist 2 - Partially met 3 - Fully met 4 - Exceeds	Question 2 How much will a change in this indicator improve the health and safety of students and staff? 1 - Very little 2 - Some 3 - Quite a bit 4 - A lot	Question 3 How much effort will it take to significantly change the current status of this indicator? 1 - Very little 2 - Some 3 - A lot 4 - Overwhelming
1. Cafeteria Meal Quality			
a. Meals offered in the cafeteria meet U.S. Department of Agriculture nutritional guidelines.			
b. Meals offered in the cafeteria include a variety of tasty, appealing, and healthy foods.			
c. The cafeteria offers to students and staff foods that are low in fat, salt, and sugar.			
d. A high-quality, nutritional breakfast is available for students every day.			
2. Support for Healthy Eating			
a. Messages displayed in the cafeteria prompt and reinforce healthy food selection.			
b. Food and Nutrition Services staff members collaborate with health education teachers to teach the knowledge and skills necessary for healthy eating.			
c. Foods and beverages are not used as rewards or punishment for academic performance or behavior.			

ASCD © 2010. All Rights Reserved.

Step 2

CHARACTERISTIC 8: FOOD AND NUTRITION SERVICES *(continued)*

Description: The culture in my school supports, promotes, and reinforces healthy eating patterns and food safety for students and staff.	**Question 1** To what extent does the standard set by this indicator appear in your school? **1 -** Does not exist **2 -** Partially met **3 -** Fully met **4 -** Exceeds	**Question 2** How much will a change in this indicator improve the health and safety of students and staff? **1 -** Very little **2 -** Some **3 -** Quite a bit **4 -** A lot	**Question 3** How much effort will it take to significantly change the current status of this indicator? **1 -** Very little **2 -** Some **3 -** A lot **4 -** Overwhelming
3. Availability of Food in Schools			
a. À la carte food items offered in the cafeteria, in school vending machines, and through other venues (e.g., school stores, snack bars, concession stands) meet healthy total calorie, fat, and sugar content standards (i.e., < 200 total calories, < 35% calories from fat, < 10% calories from saturated fats, 0 trans fats, < 35% calories from total sugars, and < 200 mg salt).			
b. À la carte beverages offered in the cafeteria, in school vending machines, and through other venues (e.g., school stores, snack bars, concession stands) are limited to plain water, low-fat and nonfat milk (8 oz. portions), 100% fruit juice (4 oz. portions for elementary and middle school, 8 oz. portions for high school), and caffeine-free; sports drinks are available only to athletes.			
c. Beverages with non-nutritive sweeteners are only available at high schools, and then only after the school day.			
d. À la carte food items and beverages offered in the cafeteria, in school vending machines, and through other venues (e.g., school stores, snack bars, concession stands) are sold at prices that students can afford.			
e. No food and drink vending machines are accessible to students during regular lunch periods.			
f. The lunch period is long enough and enough serving lines are available to allow all students time to get and eat their food without rushing (i.e., at least 10 minutes at breakfast and 20 minutes at lunch once they sit down).			

 ASCD © 2010. All Rights Reserved.

Step 2

CHARACTERISTIC 8: FOOD AND NUTRITION SERVICES *(continued)*

Description: The culture in my school supports, promotes, and reinforces healthy eating patterns and food safety for students and staff.	**Question 1** To what extent does the standard set by this indicator appear in your school? **1 -** Does not exist **2 -** Partially met **3 -** Fully met **4 -** Exceeds	**Question 2** How much will a change in this indicator improve the health and safety of students and staff? **1 -** Very little **2 -** Some **3 -** Quite a bit **4 -** A lot	**Question 3** How much effort will it take to significantly change the current status of this indicator? **1 -** Very little **2 -** Some **3 -** A lot **4 -** Overwhelming
3. Availability of Food in Schools *(continued)*			
g. Parents or guardians receive nutrition and food safety guidelines for classroom snacks, sack lunches, field trips, and potlucks.			
h. School fund-raising activities involve only nonfood items or food items and beverages that meet or exceed established healthy food standards (see indicators 8.3a, 8.3b, and 8.3c above.)			
i. Any contract(s) with food and soft drink distributors stipulates that the products they provide must meet or exceed established healthy food standards (see indicators 8.3a, 8.3b, and 8.3c above).			
4. Food Safety			
a. The cafeteria is sanitary, attractive, and orderly.			
b. Foods in all venues are purchased, stored, handled, and prepared in accordance with all U.S. Department of Agriculture, state, and local food safety guidelines.			
c. Hand-washing facilities are accessible to both students and staff in or near the cafeteria.			

RESOURCES

The following resources will help you promote and reinforce healthy eating patterns and food safety for students and staff.

Action for Healthy Kids. (2004, October). *The learning connection: The value of improving nutrition and physical activity in our schools.* Retrieved from http://www.actionforhealthykids.org/resources/files/learning-connection.pdf

ASCD © 2010. All Rights Reserved.

Step 2

Caldwell, D., Nestle, M., & Rogers, W. (1998). School nutrition services. In E. Marx, S. F. Wooley, & D. Northrop (Eds.), *Health is academic: A guide to coordinated school health programs* (pp. 195–223). New York: Teachers College Press.

Center for Science in the Public Interest. (n.d.). *Healthy school snacks.* Retrieved from http://www.cspinet .org/nutritionpolicy/healthy_school_snacks.pdf

Center for Science in the Public Interest. (2007, February). *Sweet deals: School fundraising can be healthy and profitable.* Retrieved from http://cspinet.org/new/pdf/schoolfundraising.pdf

Centers for Disease Control and Prevention. (1996). Guidelines for school health programs to promote lifelong healthy eating. *Morbidity and Mortality Weekly Report: Recommendations and Reports, 46*(RR-9). Retrieved from http://www.cdc.gov/mmwr/PDF/RR/RR4509.pdf

Committee on Nutrition Standards for Foods in Schools. (2007). *Nutrition standards for foods in schools: Leading the way toward healthier youth.* Washington, DC: Institutes of Medicine of the National Academies.

Health, Mental Health and Safety Guidelines for Schools. (n.d.). *Nutrition and food services.* Retrieved from http://www.nationalguidelines.org/chapter_full.cfm?chapter=nutrition

Kessler, D. A. (2009). *The end of overeating: Taking control of the insatiable American appetite.* New York: Rodale Inc.

Miura, M. R., Smith, J. A., & Alderman, J. (2009). *Mapping school foods.* Retrieved from http://www .chefann.com/html/tools-links/cool-food-tools/mappingschoolfood.pdf

National Center for Chronic Disease Prevention and Health Promotion. (n.d.). *Health topics: Nutrition* [Home page]. Retrieved from http://www.cdc.gov/HealthyYouth/nutrition/index.htm

School Nutrition Association. (n.d.). [Home page]. Retrieved from http://www.schoolnutrition.org/

U.S. Department of Agriculture Food and Nutrition Service. (n.d.). *Local wellness policy.* Retrieved from http://www.fns.usda.gov/tn/Healthy/wellnesspolicy.html

U.S. Department of Agriculture Food and Nutrition Service. (2000). *Changing the scene: Improving the school nutrition environment.* Available from www.fns.usda.gov/tn/Resources/changing.html

U.S. Department of Agriculture Food and Nutrition Service. (2005). *Making it happen! School nutrition success stories.* Available from www.fns.usda.gov/tn/Resources/makingithappen.html

RECOMMENDED ASCD RESOURCES

Franklin, J. (2004, Winter). Shaping up at school: Programs aim to promote fitness and nutrition. *Curriculum Update.*

Health and learning. (2009). *Educational Leadership, 67*(4). Retrieved from http://www.ascd.org/ publications/educational-leadership/dec09/vol67/num04/toc.aspx

Health and physical education. (2004). *Curriculum Technology Quarterly, 14*(2).

Lewallen, T. C. (2004, August). Healthy learning environments. *ASCD InfoBrief, 38.*

Wolfe, P., Burkman, M. A., & Streng, K. (2000). The science of nutrition. *Educational Leadership, 57*(6), 57–59.

Step 2

Characteristic 9: School Health Services

Students' ability to learn and staff members' ability to do their jobs at an optimum level depend on their physical and mental health. School health services are directly linked to education and behavioral outcomes, including reduced absenteeism.

School health services include screenings and referrals to community resources as well as services to support students with special needs. They also include primary and preventive physical and mental health care. School health service providers may also be involved in health promotion and disease prevention for students and staff (Center for Health and Health Care in Schools, n.d.).

SCORING TIPS

⋯⟩ The indicators for this characteristic take into account the different models for providing school health services.

⋯⟩ Include community or public health service providers in this work group.

ASCD © 2010. All Rights Reserved.

The Healthy School Report Card

CHARACTERISTIC 9: SCHOOL HEALTH SERVICES

	Question 1 To what extent does the standard set by this indicator appear in your school? 1 - Does not exist 2 - Partially met 3 - Fully met 4 - Exceeds	Question 2 How much will a change in this indicator improve the health and safety of students and staff? 1 - Very little 2 - Some 3 - Quite a bit 4 - A lot	Question 3 How much effort will it take to significantly change the current status of this indicator? 1 - Very little 2 - Some 3 - A lot 4 - Overwhelming
Description: The culture in my school ensures student access to primary prevention, intervention, and treatment of disease and medical disorders.			
1. Staffing			
a. The ratio of school nurses to students is maintained at a minimum of 1:750 (1:225 in student populations that may require daily professional school nursing services or interventions; 1:125 in student populations with complex health care needs).			
b. School medical personnel routinely promote and reinforce healthy and safe behaviors.			
c. Key school staff members are currently trained to administer emergency first aid, including CPR.			
d. Medical procedures and medications are administered by licensed health professionals.			
e. School health services personnel monitor students who are allowed to self-administer medications.			
2. Basic Services			
a. Health services personnel routinely screen students for vision, hearing, and dental problems.			
b. Health services personnel (or their designees) routinely measure students' height and weight, calculate body mass index (BMI), and report findings with recommendations to parents.			
c. A school nurse can provide immunizations and physical assessments, as well as some medical treatments, case management, and follow-up.			

Step 2

CHARACTERISTIC 9: SCHOOL HEALTH SERVICES *(continued)*

Description: The culture in my school ensures student access to primary prevention, intervention, and treatment of disease and medical disorders.	**Question 1** To what extent does the standard set by this indicator appear in your school? **1** - Does not exist **2** - Partially met **3** - Fully met **4** - Exceeds	**Question 2** How much will a change in this indicator improve the health and safety of students and staff? **1** - Very little **2** - Some **3** - Quite a bit **4** - A lot	**Question 3** How much effort will it take to significantly change the current status of this indicator? **1** - Very little **2** - Some **3** - A lot **4** - Overwhelming
2. Basic Services *(continued)*			
d. Health services personnel communicate with teachers regarding the health needs of students on a confidential, case-by-case, need-to-know basis.			
e. Health services personnel act as a resource to the health education curriculum.			
f. Current complete, confidential, computerized health records (including required physical exam results and immunization information) are maintained on every enrolled student.			
g. A current emergency card for every student is on file.			
h. The health status of students with chronic illness (e.g., diabetes, asthma, allergies, obesity, eating disorders, hemophilia, cancer) is routinely monitored.			
i. On-site health services are provided for students with special needs.			
j. Student attendance records are routinely monitored to identify health-related causes of absences.			
k. Prescription and over-the-counter medications are stored and administered in accordance with state law.			
l. The school has a separate, private, and well-equipped health facility (e.g., sink, bed, computer, locked file cabinet, locked medical cabinet, proper waste containers).			
m. Students are referred to community-based medical and dental facilities, as needed.			

Step 2

ASCD © 2010. All Rights Reserved.

CHARACTERISTIC 9: SCHOOL HEALTH SERVICES *(continued)*

Description: The culture in my school ensures student access to primary prevention, intervention, and treatment of disease and medical disorders.	**Question 1** To what extent does the standard set by this indicator appear in your school? **1** - Does not exist **2** - Partially met **3** - Fully met **4** - Exceeds	**Question 2** How much will a change in this indicator improve the health and safety of students and staff? **1** - Very little **2** - Some **3** - Quite a bit **4** - A lot	**Question 3** How much effort will it take to significantly change the current status of this indicator? **1** - Very little **2** - Some **3** - A lot **4** - Overwhelming
2. Basic Services *(continued)*			
n. Child health insurance enrollment of eligible students is facilitated.			
3. Access to School-Based or School-Linked Medical Care			
a. The school has or is linked to a fully staffed medical clinic where students go for primary medical care (e.g., immunizations, physicals, examinations, treatment, follow-up) and case management.			
b. Students have access to a physician, physician's assistant, or nurse practitioner at school.			
c. Students have access to dental services at school.			

RESOURCES

The following resources will help you ensure that students have access to primary prevention, intervention, and treatment of disease and medical disorders.

American School Health Association. (n.d.). *Confidentiality of student health records.* Retrieved from http://www.ashaweb.org/i4a/pages/index.cfm?pageid=3298

Center for Health and Health Care in Schools. (2007). [Home page]. Retrieved from http://www.healthinschools.org

Dryfoos, J. G. (1994). *Full service schools: A revolution in health and social services for children, youth, and families.* San Francisco: Jossey-Bass.

Duncan, P., & Igoe, J. B. (1988). School health services. In E. Marx, S. F. Wooley, & D. Northrop (Eds.), *Health is academic: A guide to coordinated school health programs* (pp. 169–194). New York: Teachers College Press.

Health, Mental Health and Safety Guidelines for Schools. (n.d.). *Health and mental health services.* Retrieved from http://www.nationalguidelines.org/chapter_full.cfm?chapter=mentalHealth

National Assembly on School-Based Health Care. (n.d.). [Home page]. Retrieved from http://www .nasbhc.org

National Center for Chronic Disease Prevention and Health Promotion. (2010). *Strategies for addressing asthma within a coordinated school health program.* Retrieved from http://www.cdc.gov/HealthyYouth/ asthma/strategies.htm

National Diabetes Education Program. (n.d.). *Teens.* Retrieved from http://www.ndep.nih.gov/diabetes/ youth/youth.htm

National Diabetes Education Program American Indian Work Group. (2006). *Move it! And reduce your risk of diabetes school kit.* Retrieved from http://www.ndep.nih.gov/media/moveit_school_kit.pdf

Nihiser, A. J., Lee, S. M., Wechsler, H., McKenna, M., Odom, E., Reinold, C., Thompson, D., & Grummer-Strawn, L. (2007). Body mass index measurement in schools. *Journal of School Health, 77*(10), 651–671. Retrieved from http://www.cdc.gov/HealthyYouth/obesity/BMI/pdf/BMI_ execsumm.pdf

Teufel, J. A. (2006). An overview of school health center sustainability from an ecological perspective. *The Health Education Monograph Series, 23,* 24–29.

RECOMMENDED ASCD RESOURCES

Maguire, S. (2000). A community school. *Educational Leadership, 57*(6), 18–21.

Marx, E., & Northrop, D. (2000). Partnerships to keep students healthy. *Educational Leadership, 57*(6), 22–24.

Wooley, S. F., Eberst, R. M., & Bradley, B. J. (2000). Creative collaborations with health providers. *Educational Leadership, 57*(6), 25–28.

Step 2

ASCD © 2010. All Rights Reserved.

The Healthy School Report Card

 # Characteristic 10: Counseling, Psychological, and Social Services

An integrated approach to counseling, psychological, and social services helps develop emotionally healthy students and reduce barriers to learning. Coordination of services provides a continuum of programming that addresses the needs of all students. Service providers also coordinate intervention and treatment programs for students with behavioral, substance abuse, and mental health problems. Through this staff, teachers may receive consultation on dealing with student mental health issues. Staff also provides services to students with special needs, facilitating their inclusion in class and school activities (Brener, Martindale, & Weist, 2001).

SCORING TIPS

----> Include community-based service providers in this work group.
----> Some indicators differ by grade-level guidelines.

Step 2

ASCD © 2010. All Rights Reserved.

CHARACTERISTIC 10: COUNSELING, PSYCHOLOGICAL, AND SOCIAL SERVICES

Description: The culture in my school ensures student access to primary prevention, intervention, and treatment of mental health and substance abuse problems.	**Question 1** To what extent does the standard set by this indicator appear in your school? **1** - Does not exist **2** - Partially met **3** - Fully met **4** - Exceeds	**Question 2** How much will a change in this indicator improve the health and safety of students and staff? **1** - Very little **2** - Some **3** - Quite a bit **4** - A lot	**Question 3** How much effort will it take to significantly change the current status of this indicator? **1** - Very little **2** - Some **3** - A lot **4** - Overwhelming
1. Staffing			
a. The ratio of students to professional counselors is maintained at a minimum of 250:1.			
2. Classroom Support			
a. Mental health staff members assist with the development and classroom implementation of the social and emotional learning lessons of the health curriculum.			
b. Mental health staff members assist teachers in determining the best behavioral interventions for chronically disruptive students.			
3. Support and Intervention Services			
a. Students are periodically assessed for social and emotional development.			
b. Early intervention is provided for students who may have mental health or substance abuse problems, including the potential to commit violent acts.			
c. Staff members are trained in early identification of signs of deteriorating behavior or academic problems indicative of mental health or substance abuse problems.			
d. A team of mental health and health services professionals recommends interventions or alternative placements for students with behavior or learning problems.			

Step 2

ASCD © 2010. All Rights Reserved.

CHARACTERISTIC 10: COUNSELING, PSYCHOLOGICAL, AND SOCIAL SERVICES *(continued)*

Description: The culture in my school ensures student access to primary prevention, intervention, and treatment of mental health and substance abuse problems.	**Question 1** To what extent does the standard set by this indicator appear in your school? **1** - Does not exist **2** - Partially met **3** - Fully met **4** - Exceeds	**Question 2** How much will a change in this indicator improve the health and safety of students and staff? **1** - Very little **2** - Some **3** - Quite a bit **4** - A lot	**Question 3** How much effort will it take to significantly change the current status of this indicator? **1** - Very little **2** - Some **3** - A lot **4** - Overwhelming
3. Support and Intervention Services *(continued)*			
e. Support groups are provided for students dealing with personal issues that interfere with learning (e.g., family conflict, parental divorce, parental substance abuse and addiction, stress, grief and loss, teen parenting, weight problems, eating disorders, smoking cessation).			
f. Students who are at risk have access to on-site mental health or case management services, including social worker and probation officer support.			
4. Appropriate and Constructive Discipline-Related Intervention			
a. Students who violate the student code of conduct due to tobacco, alcohol, or other drug use; violence; bullying; intimidation; and harassment can volunteer to attend intensive school-based intervention programs instead of suspension.			
b. Students who commit tobacco-related offenses are subject to alternative methods of discipline, such as community service or monetary fines, instead of suspension.			
c. Students at risk of alcohol and other drug dependency, committing violent acts, or mental health problems are referred to community agencies for assessment and treatment.			
5. Crisis Management			
a. A crisis team manages emergencies such as drug overdose, injury, or death of a student or staff member in accordance with an established crisis management plan.			

Step 2

Step 2

CHARACTERISTIC 10: COUNSELING, PSYCHOLOGICAL, AND SOCIAL SERVICES *(continued)*

Description: The culture in my school ensures student access to primary prevention, intervention, and treatment of mental health and substance abuse problems.	**Question 1** To what extent does the standard set by this indicator appear in your school?	**Question 2** How much will a change in this indicator improve the health and safety of students and staff?	**Question 3** How much effort will it take to significantly change the current status of this indicator?
	1 - Does not exist **2 -** Partially met **3 -** Fully met **4 -** Exceeds	**1 -** Very little **2 -** Some **3 -** Quite a bit **4 -** A lot	**1 -** Very little **2 -** Some **3 -** A lot **4 -** Overwhelming
5. Crisis Management *(continued)*			
b. Community-based mental health professionals assist with crisis events.			

RESOURCES

The following resources will help you ensure student access to primary prevention, intervention, and treatment of mental health and substance abuse problems.

Adelman, H. (1998). School counseling, psychological, and social services. In E. Marx, S. F. Wooley, & D. Northrop (Eds.), *Health is academic: A guide to coordinated school health programs* (pp. 142–168). New York: Teachers College Press.

American School Counselor Association. (n.d.). *National model for school counseling programs.* Retrieved from http://www.ascanationalmodel.org

American School Counselor Association. (2009). *The role of the professional school counselor.* Retrieved from http://www.schoolcounselor.org/content.asp?pl=133&sl=240&contentid=240

Anderson, M. B., Crowley, J. F., Herzog, C. L., & Wenger, S. (2007). *Help is down the hall: A handbook on student assistance.* Rockville, MD: Center for Substance Abuse Prevention, Substance Abuse and Mental Health Services Administration. Retrieved from http://www.nacoa.net/pdfs/SAP%20HANDBOOK .pdf

Center for Health and Health Care in Schools. (2007). [Home page]. Retrieved from http://www.health inschools.org

Center for School Mental Health Assistance at University of Maryland School of Medicine. (n.d.). *CSMH: Advancing effective school mental health* [Home page]. Retrieved from http://csmh.umaryland.edu/

Health, Mental Health and Safety Guidelines for Schools. (n.d.). *Health and mental health services.* Retrieved from http://www.nationalguidelines.org/chapter_full.cfm?chapter=mentalHealth

UCLA School Mental Health Project. (n.d.). [Home page]. Retrieved from http://smhp.psych.ucla.edu

ASCD © 2010. All Rights Reserved.

RECOMMENDED ASCD RESOURCES

The adolescent learner. (2005). *Educational Leadership, 62*(7).

Creating caring schools. (2003). *Educational Leadership, 60*(6).

Eichel, J., Goldman, L., & Kaufman, F. (Presenters). (2004). *Shaping powerful learning by promoting mental and emotional health* [Audio recording]. Alexandria, VA: ASCD.

Characteristic 11: School-Site Health Promotion for Staff

School-site health promotion for staff members can reduce absenteeism, increase productivity, and improve their quality of life as well as reduce health care costs and increase retention rates. Staff participation in healthy behaviors serves as a model for students. School-site health promotion encompasses physical and mental health programs, including those that prevent disease and disability. Health screenings, fitness programs, health education, and employee assistance programs are also part of a quality staff health promotion program (Grunbaum, Rutman, & Sathrum, 2001).

SCORING TIPS

→ When assessing if all staff members have the opportunity to participate in wellness activities, check your school's policies and practices to see if the activities and services are open to everyone who works in your school.

→ Health insurance providers and school district risk managers are often good allies for developing staff wellness programs and could be valuable participants for this group work.

ASCD © 2010. All Rights Reserved.

CHARACTERISTIC 11: SCHOOL-SITE HEALTH PROMOTION FOR STAFF

Description: The culture in my school ensures high-level job performance and healthy role models for students by supporting and facilitating the physical and mental health and well-being of all employees.	**Question 1** To what extent does the standard set by this indicator appear in your school? **1 -** Does not exist **2 -** Partially met **3 -** Fully met **4 -** Exceeds	**Question 2** How much will a change in this indicator improve the health and safety of students and staff? **1 -** Very little **2 -** Some **3 -** Quite a bit **4 -** A lot	**Question 3** How much effort will it take to significantly change the current status of this indicator? **1 -** Very little **2 -** Some **3 -** A lot **4 -** Overwhelming
1. Health Promotion Programming			
a. All staff members have opportunities to participate in on-site physical activity programs.			
b. All staff members have opportunities to regularly participate in self-improvement activities on health-related topics (e.g., stress management, nutrition, weight management, smoking cessation, personal planning, safety, and first aid).			
c. All staff can participate in basic health screenings (e.g., health risk appraisal, blood pressure, blood lipids, height and weight).			
d. Incentives and rewards (e.g., prizes, cost reimbursement, compensation for unused sick days) are used to motivate staff members' participation in health activities.			
e. The health promotion program is planned by a committee representing all employee classifications and collective bargaining units.			
f. A survey of staff members' wellness programming interests, preferred modes of program delivery, and availability to participate is conducted annually.			
g. A calendar of health promotion programming is provided to employees at least once per month.			
h. A planned marketing campaign, including a unique logo, is implemented to encourage employee participation.			
i. The employee health and disability insurance carrier provides funds, materials, and other resources for the employee health promotion program.			

CHARACTERISTIC 11: SCHOOL-SITE HEALTH PROMOTION FOR STAFF *(continued)*

Description: The culture in my school ensures high-level job performance and healthy role models for students by supporting and facilitating the physical and mental health and well-being of all employees.	**Question 1** To what extent does the standard set by this indicator appear in your school? **1** - Does not exist **2** - Partially met **3** - Fully met **4** - Exceeds	**Question 2** How much will a change in this indicator improve the health and safety of students and staff? **1** - Very little **2** - Some **3** - Quite a bit **4** - A lot	**Question 3** How much effort will it take to significantly change the current status of this indicator? **1** - Very little **2** - Some **3** - A lot **4** - Overwhelming
1. Health Promotion Programming *(continued)*			
j. Local health providers (e.g., hospitals, clinics, HMOs, voluntary health organizations) collaborate in the staff health promotion program.			
k. Special discounts for school employees are arranged with community-based physical fitness and health-promotion organizations.			
2. Employee Assistance Program			
a. An ongoing information campaign is implemented to inform employees about the employee assistance program and how to voluntarily access employee assistance program services.			
b. All staff members can receive from an outside agency short-term, confidential assistance with personal problems at no cost to them.			
c. As part of a plan of assistance, staff members with deteriorating work performance can be required to attend short-term, confidential, personal counseling at no cost to them.			

RESOURCES

The following resources will help you ensure high-level job performance and healthy role models for students by supporting and facilitating the physical and mental health and well-being of all employees.

Allegrante, J. P. (1998). School-site health promotion for staff. In E. Marx, S. F. Wooley, & D. Northrop (Eds.), *Health is academic: A guide to coordinated school health programs* (pp. 224–243). New York: Teachers College Press.

© 2010. All Rights Reserved.

Directors of Health Promotion and Education. (2007). *School employee wellness: A guide for protecting the assets of our nation's schools.* Available from http://www.schoolempwell.org/

Health, Mental Health and Safety Guidelines for Schools. (n.d.). *Staff health and safety.* Retrieved from http://www.nationalguidelines.org/chapter_full.cfm?chapter=staff

RECOMMENDED ASCD RESOURCES

Allen, R. (2004, Winter). Keeping teachers healthy: Staff wellness program yields results. *Curriculum Update.*

Davies, J., Davies, R., & Heacock, J. (2003). *Educational Leadership, 60*(8), 68–70.

Kiernan, L. J. (Producer). (1997). *How to reduce stress in your school* [Videotape]. Alexandria, VA: ASCD.

Step 2

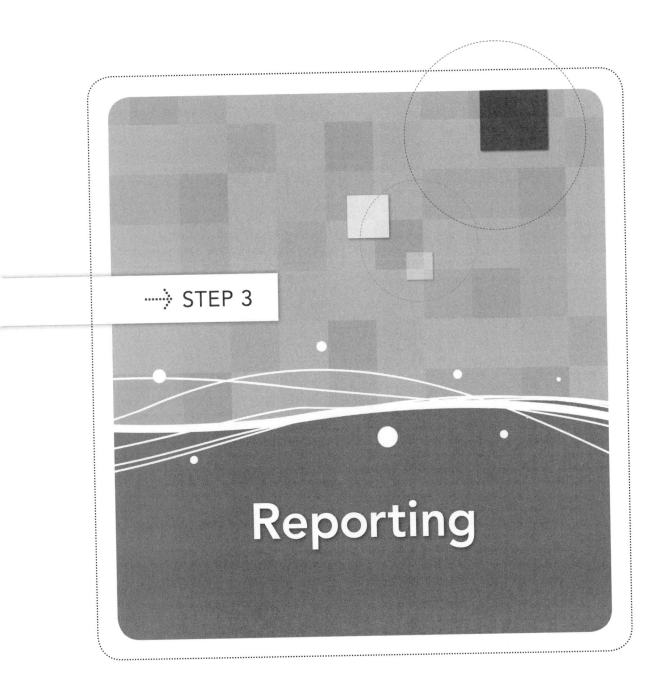

STEP 3

Reporting

Reporting the Data

At this point, you should have the Healthy School Report Card color-coded results summary that was generated by the ASCD online software. This next step covers the activities your work group will carry out in preparation for making the full set of recommendations.

PREPARING WORK GROUP SUMMARY REPORTS

Each work group should use the color-coded results summary for its report card characteristic(s) as a guide to help prepare a work group summary report. The report for each characteristic should include the following:

- Existing strengths (all indicators with no color).
- Recommendations for improvement (all indicators assigned a color, beginning with those that are green indicating short-term, high-priority actions).
- Resources (documents and other materials, such as those listed in this manual, that will guide implementation of the highest-quality policies, programs, and services).

The groups should use the sample format included in this action tool (see "Sample Work Group Report Format" on page 145) or, if needed, a format developed by the steering committee. A standardized report format can save the work groups some time and effort because each work group's report can be more easily interpreted by others and multiple work group reports can be more readily condensed for an overall summary report.

SHARE SUMMARY REPORTS ACROSS WORK GROUPS

So that all participants gain a perspective on all aspects of the report card, establish a method to share each group's summary report with members of all other work groups. You can do this through a variety of formats. Some suggestions include holding a joint meeting using formal presentations or a series of round table presentations or discussions in small groups.

 © 2010. All Rights Reserved.

Step 3

Or, you may choose to distribute printed copies with a series of questions for feedback. Work group participants should have opportunities to ask questions and provide comments on the reports prepared by other groups.

DRAFTING AN OVERALL SUMMARY REPORT

The steering committee should use the work group reports to develop a full summary report. The summary report should highlight the positive aspects of your school's health programming as well as those aspects that need to be improved. The report should also make it clear that the process of becoming a health-promoting school is ongoing and continuous.

Similar to the work group reports, the summary report could include the following sections:

- A description of the process, including examples of how you collected the information to score the report card and a summary of the report card ratings for all characteristics and indicators.
- Overall conclusions that can be drawn about the school related to each of the characteristics and associated indicators.
- Recommendations for actions that should be taken to improve the health-promoting characteristics of your school.
- Interpretations of the data, including the priority ranking of recommendations based on the potential impact each recommendation will have on student and staff health and safety, the amount of effort required to fully address each recommendation, and the potential to generate support and resources for each recommendation.
- A fully scored report card as an appendix to the report.

DISSEMINATING THE REPORT

A chief benefit of completing the report card should be to celebrate the health and safety program accomplishments of your school and to raise awareness about the aspects of your program that need improvement. To accomplish both of these aims, you should share the report card summary report widely with your school stakeholders; your school district decision makers; and the broader community, including school faculty and staff, parents, students, the superintendent and other central administrators, school board members, community health and social service agencies representatives, and members of the media. Some ideas for dissemination include

- Distribution of the entire final report.
- Distribution of an executive summary in brochure form.

Step 3

ASCD © 2010. All Rights Reserved.

- Distribution of a press release.
- Formal presentations by a cross section of designated, prepared spokespersons.
- School and community discussion forum.

Acknowledge the contributions of all steering committee members and work group members during the dissemination process, and consider creating opportunities for steering committee members and work group members to serve as spokespersons.

Be sure to thank your work group and steering committee members for all their work. Consider sending periodic updates to let them know what progress is being made on implementing the recommendations they put forward.

RECOMMENDED ASCD RESOURCE

Smith, J. (2003). *Education and public health: Natural partners in learning for life*. Alexandria, VA: ASCD.

ASCD © 2010. All Rights Reserved.

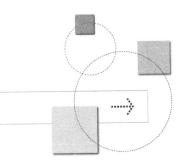

Tools for Reporting

Step 3

ASCD © 2010. All Rights Reserved.   □ 139

Developing Work Group Summary Reports

Distribute a copy of these tools to each group chair.

Objective:
Distribute and explain the color-coded output document from the online analysis tool at a work group meeting.

Activity	Person Responsible	Completion Date	Evidence of Completion

Step 3

ASCD © 2010. All Rights Reserved.

Objective:
Within each work group, use the color-coded output to generate lists of strengths and potential areas of improvement for each characteristic.

Activity	Person Responsible	Completion Date	Evidence of Completion

ASCD © 2010. All Rights Reserved.

Step 3

Tools for Reporting

Objective:
Review the draft work group reports for accuracy by consulting internal and external experts and revise as needed.

Activity	Person Responsible	Completion Date	Evidence of Completion

Step 3

ASCD © 2010. All Rights Reserved.

Objective:
Submit work group reports to the steering committee after gaining consensus approval.

Activity	Person Responsible	Completion Date	Evidence of Completion

ASCD © 2010. All Rights Reserved.

Step 3

Sample Work Group Report Format

Copy and distribute this sample report outline for each work group.

Name of characteristic

Work group participants (name, affiliation)

Assessment process
- What method or methods did you use to collect the data? How did you choose these methods?
- If you used a survey, focus group, or interviews, how did you determine who to talk to?
- If you used a document review, list the documents included in your review.
- What challenges did you find? What opportunities did the process reveal?

Recommendations
- What outcomes did you find?
- What conclusions did you draw for the indicators and the characteristic? What areas are high-quality? Which need improvement?
- What recommendations were made by the data analysis program?
- What recommendations does the work group have for the steering committee?

Attach a copy of your completed score sheet and a copy of your data analysis report.

ASCD © 2010. All Rights Reserved.

Sharing Work Group Summary Reports

Copy these tools for each work group chair and for steering committee members to use for record keeping.

Objective:
Include the school district- or school-specific information in the introduction of the compiled Healthy School Report Card report.

Activity	Person Responsible	Completion Date	Evidence of Completion

ASCD © 2010. All Rights Reserved.

Step 3

Tools for Reporting

Objective:
Compile the completed report that includes the introduction, sections covering every indicator, and appropriate supporting documentation and prepare an executive summary.

Activity	Person Responsible	Completion Date	Evidence of Completion

Step 3

ASCD © 2010. All Rights Reserved.

Objective:
Conduct a joint meeting of the steering committee and all work group members to review the report and executive summary.

Activity	Person Responsible	Completion Date	Evidence of Completion

ASCD © 2010. All Rights Reserved.

Step 3

Objective:
Conduct follow-up, including revisions to the summary report, acknowledgements, and so forth.

Activity	Person Responsible	Completion Date	Evidence of Completion

Step 3

Objective:
Print and duplicate the report and executive summary.

Activity	Person Responsible	Completion Date	Evidence of Completion

ASCD © 2010. All Rights Reserved.

Step 3

Disseminating the Summary Report

Use these tools to organize and track dissemination strategies.

Objective: Using appropriate dissemination strategies and spokespersons, distribute the report to identified key audiences.			
Activity	**Person Responsible**	**Completion Date**	**Evidence of Completion**

ASCD © 2010. All Rights Reserved.

Objective: Gauge solicited and collected reactions to the report.			
Activity	**Person Responsible**	**Completion Date**	**Evidence of Completion**

ASCD © 2010. All Rights Reserved.

Step 3

Objective:
Capture additional offers of assistance or requests to participate in a coordinated school health program.

Activity	Person Responsible	Completion Date	Evidence of Completion

ASCD © 2010. All Rights Reserved.

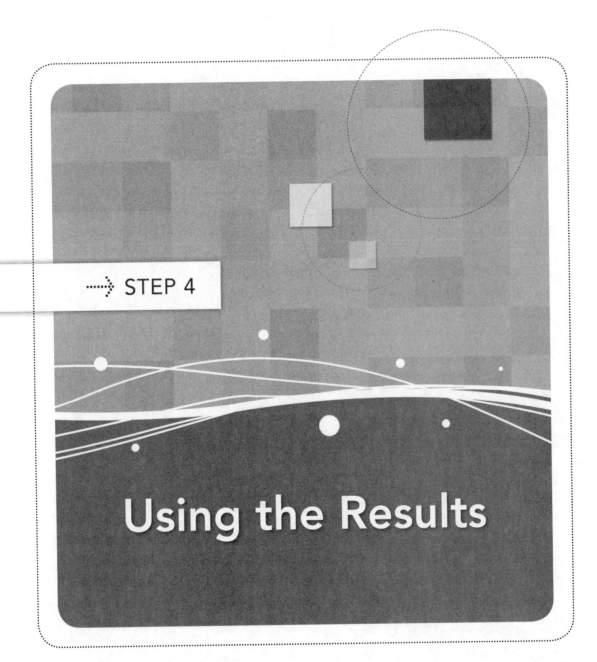

STEP 4

Using the Results

Using the Results of the Healthy School Report Card

After you have disseminated your overall summary report, gather the comments you received. Through this feedback, you may be able to identify individuals or community agencies that can assist you in developing your Healthy School Improvement Plan.

DEVELOPING A PLAN BASED ON PRIORITIZED RECOMMENDATIONS

Once you have presented the Healthy School Report Card summary report to the appropriate authority—your administrator, the school board, the community—determine whether you will develop a distinct Healthy School Improvement Plan or incorporate your recommendations into your existing school improvement plan.

To develop a Healthy School Improvement Plan, reconvene the steering committee and characteristic work groups. The overall goal should be to develop the highest-quality programs and services possible (as defined by Healthy School Report Card Characteristics 3–11) based on research findings and best practices and then coordinate them (as defined by Healthy School Report Card Characteristics 1–2). *This requires broad-based participation both for planning and in implementation, and it cannot be done by one individual or even a small group.* Be sure to involve principals, health education teachers, physical education teachers, students, parents, and others in these efforts; based on feedback from previous Healthy School Report Card users, that is one aspect that they wish they had done better.

An additional benefit of involving various stakeholder groups in preparing the plan is that the process automatically generates buy-in and support for implementation and helps secure the resources you need to make necessary improvements. You won't have to expend much additional time or effort convincing stakeholders to support the plan.

Step 4

The plan objectives should be based on the prioritized recommendations from the summary report, and they should also include

- Specific steps for completing each objective.
- Time lines for completing objectives.
- Assigned leadership responsibilities.
- Evaluation criteria to determine if objectives are met.
- Required resources as well as the sources of resources.

USING PLANNING CHARTS

As with the Healthy School Report Card summary report, the Healthy School Communities website provides a planning form for every indicator, identifying the associated Healthy School Report Card characteristic and provides a suitable objective. In the fields below the objective, the work groups can check the priority of each objective and whether it should be completed in the short term or the long term. You should derive both objective priority and short- or long-term status from your color-coded report card results summary. Once you've checked these fields, work groups should insert

- Activities that should be completed to achieve the objective.
- Resources required to achieve the objective.
- Individuals or groups responsible for seeing that the objective is attained.
- The projected completion date.
- Evidence that the objective has been attained.

Based on local needs and practices, your work groups may decide to consolidate objectives or configure the plan in some other way. Regardless of how you develop the plan, you should use the color-coded Healthy School Report Card results summary to inform your decisions.

Schools have found that using a two-tiered approach of short-term and long-term objectives has several advantages. When people volunteer to get involved, they often want to "do" and are not long or easily satisfied by engaging in planning (regardless of how important sound planning is to long-term success). With short-term objectives, these volunteers can complete tasks while others engage in more involved development of long-term objectives.

Also, by completing several short-term objectives, all those involved can achieve and demonstrate successes quickly. You can use these early successes to generate publicity and, thereby, promote the overall effort and attract additional participation and support. If you choose

ASCD © 2010. All Rights Reserved.

Step 4

not to use the short-term planning forms, your plan should still include a mix of meaningful short- and long-term priority objectives.

After you have thoroughly reviewed your Healthy School Report Card results, complete the planning charts. Pay special attention to report card results for indicators that show that initiation or improvement will help you accrue substantial health benefit for students and staff.

Develop objectives that parallel Healthy School Report Card indicators. For example, the program improvement objective for Characteristic 2: Coordination of School Health Programs indicator 1d (A designated staff member [e.g., administrator, nurse, teacher, counselor] is responsible for ensuring coordination of health programs.) could be to hire a full-time school health coordinator.

TRACKING YOUR PROGRESS

Like any school improvement process, the Healthy School Report Card is an iterative process. Decide how frequently your school will assess its school health programming, and institute a mechanism for ensuring that your Healthy School Improvement Plan is being carried out. Set regular tracking and communication points to determine that you are accomplishing the objectives and that your goal of becoming a health-promoting school is attained, and celebrate successes along the way.

Step 4

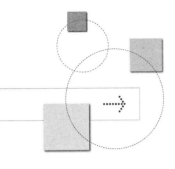

Tools for Using the Results

Step 4

ASCD © 2010. All Rights Reserved. □ 161

Developing Plans

Use these tools to track your progress.

Objective: Involve previous and new members of work groups in the preparation of a Healthy School Improvement Plan.			
Activity	**Person Responsible**	**Completion Date**	**Evidence of Completion**

Step 4

ASCD © 2010. All Rights Reserved.

Objective:
Using the Healthy School Report Card report and color-coded output document, finalize the prioritized actions for every characteristic and categorize them by level of importance and urgency.

Activity	Person Responsible	Completion Date	Evidence of Completion

Step 4

ASCD © 2010. All Rights Reserved.

Objective:
Develop a Healthy School Improvement Plan document based directly on the color-coded output from the Healthy School Report Card online analysis tool.

Activity	Person Responsible	Completion Date	Evidence of Completion

ASCD © 2010. All Rights Reserved.

Tools for Using the Results

Objective: Using appropriate dissemination strategies and spokespersons, distribute the Healthy School Improvement Plan to identified key audiences.			
Activity	**Person Responsible**	**Completion Date**	**Evidence of Completion**

ASCD © 2010. All Rights Reserved.

Step 4

Tools for Using the Results

Objective:
Implement your Healthy School Improvement Plan over time.

Activity	Person Responsible	Completion Date	Evidence of Completion

Step 4

ASCD © 2010. All Rights Reserved.

Healthy School Improvement Plan Chart

For each indicator in the Healthy School Report Card, fill out a separate planning template. Pay special attention to indicators whose results in the color-coded report card analysis show that, if initiated or improved, you can accrue substantial health benefit for students or staff.

Plan objectives should be measurable and parallel the indicators of the Healthy School Report Card. For example, the program improvement objective for Characteristic 2's indicator 1d (A designated staff member [e.g., administrator, nurse, teacher, counselor] is responsible for assuring coordination of health programs.) could be "Hire a full-time school health coordinator."

Characteristic:

Indicator:

Objective:

Priority time:
☐ Short Term ☐ Long Term

Priority level:
☐ High ☐ Medium ☐ Low

Activities	Resources	Individual or Group Responsible	Completion Date	Evidence of Completion

ASCD © 2010. All Rights Reserved.

Step 4

Track Your Progress

Copy these tools for the facilitator of the Healthy School Communities process or the school health coordinator to use to assess the progress of your school improvement plan implementation.

Objective: Use a formal tracking system to record progress on implementing your Healthy School Improvement Plan and identify midcourse corrections.			
Activity	**Person Responsible**	**Completion Date**	**Evidence of Completion**

Step 4

Objective:

Document accomplishments and achievements related to implementing your Healthy School Improvement Plan.

Activity	Person Responsible	Completion Date	Evidence of Completion

Step 4

ASCD © 2010. All Rights Reserved.

Objective:
Using appropriate dissemination strategies and spokespersons, publicize accomplishments, achievements, and benefits associated with implementing your Healthy School Improvement Plan.

Activity	Person Responsible	Completion Date	Evidence of Completion

Step 4

Objective:
Celebrate participation and successes.

Activity	Person Responsible	Completion Date	Evidence of Completion

ASCD © 2010. All Rights Reserved.

Step 4

Appendix

Methodology

The developers of the Healthy School Report Card took measures to ensure the methodology used to create the report card was both valid and reliable.

VALIDITY

The initial characteristics for the Healthy School Report Card were selected using the Coordinated School Health Program Model developed by Lloyd Kolbe and Diane Allensworth and promulgated by the U.S. Department of Health and Human Services Centers for Disease Control and Prevention's Division of Adolescent and School Health. This model was the starting point, followed by an extensive review of literature from across a variety of disciplines resulting in the addition of two characteristics: (1) School Health Program Policy and Strategic Planning and (2) Coordination of School Health Programs. The literature also supported the division of the "school environment" into two separate constructs—the social and emotional school climate and the physical environment, including safety.

During the literature review, a matrix was used to track consistency across and within disciplines of the indicators that promote positive health, behavior, and achievement outcomes in the school and in individual classrooms. In August 2003, the draft list of characteristics and indicators was presented at a meeting of a panel of national experts for review and discussion. Panelists' recommendations were incorporated in the first round of revisions to the draft characteristics and indicators.

Following the expert panel meeting, the indicators were compared with the draft U.S. National Guidelines on Health, Mental Health, and Safety to ensure consistency, particularly in areas where limited research exists. Based on expert panel input, the original assessment scale was changed to one developed by Robert Marzano for ASCD's What Works in Schools®

ASCD © 2010. All Rights Reserved.

Appendix

program. The scale used in the Healthy School Report Card was further refined after a field test.

In March 2004, three focus groups provided input and feedback for the proposed assessment tool and implementation process then called the ASCD Healthy School Report Card with Guidance. ASCD randomly selected and invited 150 members who were registered to attend the association's annual conference and who met specified criteria. Invitees needed to be either a principal or a superintendent at the time the focus groups were held. The selection process included methods for ensuring diversity based on geographic location and type of district (urban, rural, or suburban). A consultant not previously associated with the development of the report card facilitated the groups. The feedback elicited through the focus groups was used to further revise some of the language used to describe the Healthy School Report Card and to refine the process and the guidance.

Beginning in April 2004, a field test of the Healthy School Report Card with Guidance was conducted in Indiana. School representatives attended a full-day training session on its use and their role as pilot test schools. Of the 10 schools originally interested in participating in the field test, 4 completed the process and provided feedback. This feedback was used to refine the language in the original scales and to make the Healthy School Report Card with Guidance more user-friendly. When field test schools expressed concerns about the content of the report card, the literature was used to confirm the items' importance to developing and maintaining a high-functioning, health-promoting school. Rather than eliminating the indicators, strategies were added in the guidance to address the concerns the field test schools raised.

The final format of *Creating a Healthy School Using the Healthy School Report Card: An ASCD Action Tool* was selected based on recommendations from an ASCD staff team.

RELIABILITY

After the field test, teams from 39 schools within 10 Indiana and 8 Michigan school districts rated their health programs using the entire Healthy School Report Card. An algorithm was developed to provide guidance to schools on short-term and long-term priorities for action. Schools reported on using the process for developing action plans and for bringing together stakeholders to address their school's health programming.

ASCD © 2010. All Rights Reserved.

Methodology

For each of the 11 report card characteristics, which range from 9–26 indicators each, Chronbach's Alpha was calculated using the data provided by the 39 schools. Cronbach's Alpha is one method of estimating how reliable survey items are when they are answered by different individuals over time. This statistical analysis, resulting in a coefficient of reliability, indicates the extent to which responses to the questions are consistent and stable (Aday, 1989). The higher the score, the more reliable the survey questions are estimated to be. Generally a score of 0.7 is considered an acceptable coefficient of reliability (Windsor, 1994). For all 11 characteristics, Chronbach's Alpha was equal to or greater than 0.9.

References

Aberg, M. A., Pedersen, N. L., Toren, K., Svartengren, M., Backstrand, B., Johnsson, T., . . . Kuhn, H. G. (2009). Cardiovascular fitness is associated with cognition in young adulthood. *Proceedings of the National Academy of Sciences, 106*(49), 20906. doi:10.1073/pnas.0905307106

Aday, L. A. (1989). *Designing and conducting health surveys: A comprehensive guide* (1st ed.). San Francisco: Jossey-Bass, Inc.

Arthur, M. W., Brown, E. C., & Briney, J. S. (2006, July). *Multilevel examination of the relationships between risk/protective factors and academic test scores.* Retrieved from http://www1.dshs.wa.gov/pdf/ hrsa/dasa/ResearchReports/MERRPFATS0706.pdf

ASCD. (2007). *The learning compact redefined: A call to action.* Retrieved from http://www.wholechild education.org/resources/Learningcompact7-07.pdf

Blum, R. W. (2005). A case for school connectedness. *Educational Leadership, 62*(7), 16–20.

Brener, N. D., Martindale, J., & Weist, M. D. (2001). Mental health and social services: Results from the school health policies and programs study 2000. *Journal of School Health, 71*(7), 305–312.

California Department of Education. (1999). *Getting results: Developing safe and healthy kids, update 1.* Retrieved from http://www.cde.ca.gov/ls/he/at/documents/getresultsupdate1.pdf

Castelli, D. M., Hillman, C. H., Buck, S. M., & Erwin, H. E. (2007). Physical fitness and academic achievement in third- and fifth-grade students. *Journal of Sport and Exercise Psychology, 29*, 239–252.

Center for Health and Health Care in Schools. (n.d.). *Health in schools.* Retrieved from http://www .healthinschools.org/en/Health-in-Schools.aspx

Centers for Disease Control and Prevention. (2006). *Obesity still a major problem.* Retrieved from http:// www.cdc.gov/nchs/pressroom/06facts/obesity03_04.htm

Centers for Disease Control and Prevention. (2008, November). *Physical activity and the health of young people.* Retrieved from http://www.cdc.gov/HealthyYouth/PhysicalActivity/pdf/facts.pdf

Centers for Disease Control and Prevention. (2010a). *The association between school-based physical activity, including physical education, and academic performance.* Retrieved from http://www.cdc.gov/Healthy Youth/health_and_academics/pdf/pape_executive_summary.pdf

Centers for Disease Control and Prevention. (2010b). *Healthy youth! Student health and academic achievement.* Retrieved from www.cdc.gov/healthyyouth/health_and_academics/index.htm

Chomitz, V. R., Slining, M. M., McGowan, R. J., Mitchell, S. E., Dawson, G. F., & Hacker, K. A. (2009). Is there a relationship between physical fitness and academic achievement: Positive results from public school children in the northeastern United States. *Journal of School Health, 79*(1), 30–37.

Ciaccio, J. (2004). *Totally positive teaching: A five-stage approach to energizing students and teachers.* Alexandria, VA: ASCD.

Coe, D. P., Pivarnik, J. M., Womack, C. J., Reeves, M. J., & Malina, R. M. (2006). Effect of physical education and activity levels on academic achievement in children. *Medicine and Science in Sports and Exercise, 38,* 1515–1519.

Cohen, J., McCabe, L., Michelli, N. M., & Pikeral, T. (2009). School climate: Research, policy, practice, and teacher education. *Teachers College Record, 111*(1), 180–213.

Daley, A. J., & Ryan, J. (2000). Academic performance and participation in physical activity by secondary school adolescents. *Perceptual and Motor Skills, 91,* 531–534.

Dilley, J. (2009). *Research review: School-based health interventions and academic achievement.* Retrieved from http://www.sboh.wa.gov/Pubs/docs/Health&AA.pdf

Dwyer, T., Blizzard, L., & Dean, K. (1996, April). Physical activity and performance in children. *Nutrition Reviews, 54*(4 pt. 2), 27–31.

Dwyer, T., Coonan, W. E., Leitch, D. R., Hetzel, B. S., & Baghurst, R. A. (1983). Investigation of the effects of daily physical activity on the health of primary school students in South Australia. *International Journal of Epidemiology, 12,* 308–313.

Dwyer, T., Sallis, J. F., Blizzard, L., Lazarus, R., & Dean, K. (2001). Relation of academic performance to physical activity and fitness in children. *Pediatric Exercise Science, 13,* 225–237.

Field, T., Diego, M., & Sanders, C. E. (2001). Exercise is positively related to adolescents' relationships and academics. *Adolescence, 36,* 105–110.

Fiscella, K., & Kitzman, H. (2009). Disparities in academic achievement and health: The intersection of child education and health policy. *Pediatrics, 123*(3), 1073–1080. doi:10.1542/peds.2008-0533

Grunbaum, J. A., Rutman, S. J., & Sathrum, P. R. (2001). Faculty and staff health promotion: Results from the school health policies and programs study 2000. *Journal of School Health, 71*(1), 335–339.

Haas, S. A., & Fosse, N. E. (2008). Health and the educational attainment of adolescents: Evidence from the NLSY97. *Journal of Health and Social Behavior, 49*(2), 178–192.

Hanson, T. L., Austin, G., & Lee-Bayha, J. (2004). *Ensuring that no child is left behind: How are student health risks and resilience related to the academic progress of schools?* Retrieved from http://www.wested.org/online_pubs/hd-04-02.pdf

Hillman, C., & Castelli, D. (2009, April 1). Physical activity may strengthen children's ability to pay attention. *ScienceDaily.* Retrieved from http://www.sciencedaily.com /releases/2009/03/090331183800.htm

Hobson, A. J., Ashby, P., Malderez, A., & Tomlinson, P. (2009, January). Mentoring beginning teachers: What we know and what we don't. *Teaching and Teacher Education, 25*(1), 207–216.

Ingersoll, R., & Kralik, J. M. (2004, February). The impact of mentoring on teacher retention: What the research says. *ECS Research Review.* Retrieved from http://www.ecs.org/clearinghouse/50/36/5036.pdf

Joint Committee on National Education Standards. (1995). *National health education standards: Achieving health literacy.* Atlanta, GA: American Cancer Society.

ASCD © 2010. All Rights Reserved.

Appendix

References

Kim, H. Y., Frongillo, E. A., Han, S. S., Oh, S. Y., Kim, W. K., Jang, Y. A., Won, H. S., . . . Kim, S. H. (2003). Academic performance of Korean children is associated with dietary behaviours and physical status. *Asia Pacific Journal of Clinical Nutrition, 12*(2), 186–192.

Moran, C. (2008, March 11). Runners add a dash of fitness to school day: Morning laps may give kids a head start in class. *San Diego Union Tribune*. Retrieved from http://www.signonsandiego.com

Murray, N. G., Low, B. J., Hollis, C., Cross, A. W., & Davis, S. M. (2007). Coordinated school health programs and academic achievement: A systematic review of the literature. *Journal of School Health, 77*(9), 589–600.

Nelson, M. C., & Gordon-Larson, P. (2006). Physical activity and sedentary behavior patterns are associated with selected adolescent health risk behaviors. *Pediatrics, 117*, 1281–1290.

Pellegrini, A. D., & Smith, P. K. (1998). The nature and function of a neglected aspect of play. *Child Development, 69*(3), 577–598.

Pyle, S. A., Sharkey, J., Yetter, G., Felix, E., Furlong, M. J., & Poston, C. (2006). Fighting an epidemic: The role of schools in reducing childhood obesity. *Psychology in the Schools, 43*(3), 361–376.

Sallis, J. F., McKenzie, T. L., Kolody, B., Lewis, M., Marshall, S., & Rosengard, P. (1999). Effects of health-related physical education on academic achievement: Project SPARK. *Research Quarterly for Exercise and Sport, 70*(2), 127–134.

Shephard, R. J. (1996, April). Habitual physical activity and academic performance. *Nutrition Reviews, 54*(4 pt. 2), 32–36.

Shephard, R. J. (1997). Curricular physical activity and academic performance. *Pediatric Exercise Science, 9*(2), 113–126.

Sibley, B. A., & Etnier, J. L. (2003). The relationship between physical activity and cognition in children: A meta-analysis. *Pediatric Exercise Science, 15*(3), 243–256.

Stallings, V. A., & Yaktine, A. L. (Eds.). (2007, April). *Nutrition standards for foods in schools: Leading the way toward healthier youth*. Washington, DC: Institute of Medicine Committee of the National Academie.

Tomporowski, P. D. (2003). Cognitive and behavioral responses to acute exercise in youths: A review. *Pediatric Exercise Science, 15*(4), 348–359.

Tremblay, M. S., Inman, J. W., & Willms, J. D. (2000). The relationship between physical activity, self-esteem, and academic achievement in 12-year-old children. *Pediatric Exercise Science, 12*, 312–323.

Trost, S. G. (2007, Fall). Active education: Physical education, physical activity and academic performance. *Active Living Research Brief*. Retrieved from http://www.activelivingresearch.org/alr/alr/files/Active_Ed.pdf

Trost, S. G. (2009, Summer). Active education: Physical education, physical activity and academic performance. *Active Living Research Brief*. Retrieved from http://www.activelivingresearch.org/files/Active_Ed_Summer2009.pdf

Trudeau, F., & Shephard, R. J. (2008). Physical education, school physical activity, school sports and academic performance. *International Journal of Behavioral Nutrition and Physical Activity, 5*(10). doi:10.1186/1479-5868-5-10

Vail, K. (2006a). Is physical fitness raising grades? *Education Digest, 71*(8), 13–19.

Vail, K. (2006b). Mind and body. *American School Board Journal, 193*(3), 30–33.

 © 2010. All Rights Reserved.

Appendix

Valois, R. F. (2009). [ASCD Healthy School Communities evaluation report.]. Unpublished report.

Viadero, D. (2008). Exercise seen as priming pump for students' academic strides. *Education Week, 27*(23), 14–15.

Windsor, R., Baranowski, T., & Cutter, G. (1994). *Evaluation of health promotion, health education, and disease prevention programs* (2nd ed.). Mountain View, CA: Mayfield Publishing Company.

World Health Organization. (n.d.). *What is a health promoting school?* Retrieved from www.who.int/school_youth_health/gshi/hps/en/index.html

ASCD © 2010. All Rights Reserved.

Appendix

Resources

Action for Healthy Kids. (2004, October). *The learning connection: The value of improving nutrition and physical activity in our schools.* Retrieved from http://www.actionforhealthykids.org/resources/files/learning-connection.pdf

Adelman, H. (1998). School counseling, psychological, and social services. In E. Marx, S. F. Wooley, & D. Northrop (Eds.), *Health is academic: A guide to coordinated school health programs* (pp. 142–168). New York: Teachers College Press.

The adolescent learner. (2005). *Educational Leadership, 62*(7).

Allegrante, J. P. (1998). School-site health promotion for staff. In E. Marx, S. F. Wooley, & D. Northrop (Eds.), *Health is academic: A guide to coordinated school health programs* (pp. 224–243). New York: Teachers College Press.

Allen, R. (2004, Winter). Keeping teachers healthy: Staff wellness program yields results. *Curriculum Update.*

Allen, R. (2005). New paradigms for parental involvement: Stronger family role in schools seen as key to achievement. *Education Update, 47*(3), 3–5.

Allensworth, D., Lawson, E., Nicholson, L., & Wyche, J. (Eds.). (1997). *Schools and health: Our nation's investment.* Washington, DC: National Academy Press.

American Alliance for Health, Physical Education, Recreation and Dance: Joint Committee on National Health Education Standards. (1995). *National health education standards: For students.* Retrieved from http://www.gdoe.net/ci/hlth_ed_supp/Nat_Hlth_Ed_Std.pdf

American School Counselor Association. (n.d.). *National model for school counseling programs.* Retrieved from http://www.ascanationalmodel.org

American School Counselor Association. (2009). *The role of the professional school counselor.* Retrieved from http://www.schoolcounselor.org/content.asp?pl=133&sl=240&contentid=240

American School Health Association. (n.d.). *Confidentiality of student health records.* Retrieved from http://www.ashaweb.org/i4a/pages/index.cfm?pageid=3298

Anderson, M. B., Crowley, J. F., Herzog, C. L., & Wenger, S. (2007). *Help is down the hall: A handbook on student assistance.* Rockville, MD: Center for Substance Abuse Prevention, Substance Abuse and Mental Health Services Administration. Retrieved from http://www.nacoa.net/pdfs/SAP%20HANDBOOK.pdf

Annie E. Casey Foundation. (n.d.). *Kids count* [Home page]. Retrieved from http://www.kidscount.org

ASCD. (2007). *The learning compact redefined: A call to action*. Retrieved from http://www.wholechild education.org/resources/Learningcompact7-07.pdf

ASCD. (2009). *L2L webinar series: Creating a healthy school community*. Available from https://admin.na4 .acrobat.com/_a824650571/p65505378/

Association of State and Territorial Health Officials. (n.d.). ASTHO [Home page]. Retrieved from http:// www.astho.org

Benard, B. (n.d.). *Resilience: What we have learned*. San Francisco: WestEd.

Blank, M., & Berg, M. (2006, July). *All together now: Sharing responsibility for the whole child*. Retrieved from http://www.ascd.org/ASCD/pdf/sharingresponsibility.pdf

Blum, R. W. (2005). A case for school connectedness. *Educational Leadership, 62*(7), 16–20.

Bogden, J. F. (2000). *Fit, healthy, and ready to learn: A school health policy guide—Parts I and II*. Alexandria, VA: National Association of State Boards of Education.

Bosher, W., Kaminski, K. R., & Vacca, R. S. (2004). *The school law handbook: What every leader needs to know*. Alexandria, VA: ASCD.

Brown, J. L. (2004). *Making school improvement happen with what works in schools: School-level factors: An ASCD action tool*. Alexandria, VA: ASCD.

Building schools that build learners. (2006). *Education Update, 48*(11). Retrieved from http://www.ascd .org/publications/newsletters/education-update/nov06/vol48/num11/toc.aspx

Butterfoss, F. D., & Kegler, M. C. (2002). Toward a comprehensive understanding of community coalitions: Moving from practice to theory. In R. J. DiClemente, R. A. Crosby, & M. C. Kegler (Eds.), *Emerging theories in health promotion practice and research* (pp. 157–191). San Francisco, CA: Jossey-Bass.

Caldwell, D., Nestle, M., & Rogers, W. (1998). School nutrition services. In E. Marx, S. F. Wooley, & D. Northrop (Eds.), *Health is academic: A guide to coordinated school health programs* (pp. 195–223). New York: Teachers College Press.

Canadian Association for Health, Physical Education, Recreation and Dance. (2005). CAHPERD [Home page]. Retrieved from http://www.cahperd.ca/

Carlyon, P., Carlyon, W., & McCarthy, A. R. (1998). Family and community involvement in school health. In E. Marx, S. F. Wooley, & D. Northrop (Eds.), *Health is academic: A guide to coordinated school health programs* (pp. 67–95). New York: Teachers College Press.

CCSSO-SCASS Health Education Assessment Project. (2006). *Aligning health and reading with a HEAP of books*. Kent, OH: American School Health Association.

Center for the Education and Study of Diverse Populations at New Mexico Highlands University. (2007). *Working together: School-family-community partnerships* [Home page]. Retrieved from http://www .cesdp.nmhu.edu/toolkit/index.html

Center for Health and Health Care in Schools. (2007). [Home page]. Retrieved from http://www.health inschools.org

Center for School Mental Health Assistance at University of Maryland School of Medicine. (n.d.). *CSMH: Advancing effective school mental health* [Home page]. Retrieved from http://csmh.umaryland.edu/

Center for Science in the Public Interest. (n.d.). *Healthy school snacks*. Retrieved from http://www.cspinet .org/nutritionpolicy/healthy_school_snacks.pdf

ASCD © 2010. All Rights Reserved.

Appendix

Center for Science in the Public Interest. (2007, February). *Sweet deals: School fundraising can be healthy and profitable*. Retrieved from http://cspinet.org/new/pdf/schoolfundraising.pdf

Centers for Disease Control and Prevention. (1996). Guidelines for school health programs to promote lifelong healthy eating. *Morbidity and Mortality Weekly Report: Recommendations and Reports, 46*(RR-9). Retrieved from http://www.cdc.gov/mmwr/PDF/RR/RR4509.pdf

Centers for Disease Control and Prevention. (1997). Guidelines for school and community programs to promote lifelong physical activity among young people. *Morbidity and Mortality Weekly Report: Recommendations and Reports, 46*(RR-6). Available from http://www.cdc.gov/healthyyouth/physicalactivity/guidelines/index.htm

Centers for Disease Control and Prevention. (2008). *Make a difference at your school*. Retrieved from http://www.cdc.gov/HealthyYouth/keystrategies/pdf/make-a-difference.pdf

Centers for Disease Control and Prevention. (2010). *Division of nutrition, physical activity and obesity* [Home page]. Retrieved from http://www.cdc.gov/nccdphp/dnpa/recommendations.htm

Checkley, K. (2000, Spring). Health education: Emphasizing skills and prevention to form a more health-literate people. *Curriculum Update.*

Collaborative for High Performance Schools. (2001). *High performance schools best practices manual*. Available from http://www.chps.net/dev/Drupal/node/288

Committee on Nutrition Standards for Foods in Schools. (2007). *Nutrition standards for foods in schools: Leading the way toward healthier youth*. Washington, DC: Institutes of Medicine of the National Academies.

Communities and Schools Promoting Health. (n.d.). *Health lesson plans*. Retrieved from http://www.safehealthyschools.org/lessonplansintro.htm

Communities and Schools Promoting Health. (n.d.). *School health policies*. Retrieved from http://www.safehealthyschools.org/shpolicies/school_health_policies.htm

Council of Chief State School Officers and the Association of State and Territorial Health Officials. (2003). *The school health starter kit* (2nd ed.). Washington, DC: Council of Chief State School Officers.

Creating caring schools. (2003). *Educational Leadership, 60*(6).

Cummings, C. (2000). *Winning strategies for classroom management*. Alexandria, VA: ASCD.

Davies, J., Davies, R., & Heacock, J. (2003). *Educational Leadership, 60*(8), 68–70.

Department of Health and Human Services. (2005). *The president's council on physical fitness and sports* [Home page]. Retrieved from http://www.fitness.gov

Directors of Health Promotion and Education. (2007). *School employee wellness: A guide for protecting the assets of our nation's schools*. Available from http://www.schoolempwell.org

Dryfoos, J. G. (1994). *Full service schools: A revolution in health and social services for children, youth, and families*. San Francisco: Jossey-Bass.

Duncan, P., & Igoe, J. B. (1988). School health services. In E. Marx, S. F. Wooley, & D. Northrop (Eds.), *Health is academic: A guide to coordinated school health programs* (pp. 169–194). New York: Teachers College Press.

Egerter, S., Braveman, P., Sadegh-Nobari, T., Grossman-Kahn, R., & Dekker, M. (2009, September). Education matters for health. *Issue Brief, 6*. Retrieved from http://www.rwjf.org/files/research/commission2009eduhealth.pdf

Eichel, J., Goldman, L., & Kaufman, F. (Presenters). (2004). *Shaping powerful learning by promoting mental and emotional health* [Audio recording]. Alexandria, VA: ASCD.

Engaging the whole child. (2007). *Educational Leadership, 64*(9). Retrieved from http://www.ascd.org/ publications/educational-leadership/summer07/vol64/num09/toc.aspx

Erwin, J. C. (2004). *The classroom of choice: Giving students what they need and getting what you want.* Alexandria, VA: ASCD.

Fetro, J. V. (1998). Implementing coordinated school health programs in local schools. In E. Marx, S. F. Wooley, & D. Northrop (Eds.), *Health is academic: A guide to coordinated school health programs* (pp. 15–42). New York: Teachers College Press.

Fetro, J. V. (1998). *Step by step to health promoting schools.* Santa Cruz, CA: ETR Associates.

Franklin, J. (2004, Winter). Shaping up at school: Programs aim to promote fitness and nutrition. *Curriculum Update.*

Freiberg, H. J. (1999). *School climate: Measuring, improving and sustaining healthy learning environments.* Philadelphia, PA: Falmer Press.

Frumkin, H., Geller, R. J., & Rubin, I. L. (Eds.). (2006). *Safe and healthy school environments.* New York: Oxford University Press.

Gilman, R., Huebner, E. S., & Furlong, M. J. (2009). *Handbook of positive psychology in schools.* New York: Routledge.

Grebow, P. M., Greene, B. Z., Harvey, J., & Head, C. J. (2000). Shaping health policies. *Educational Leadership, 57*(6), 63–66.

Greene, B. Z., & McCoy, K. I. (1998). The national role in coordinated school health programs. In E. Marx, S. F. Wooley, & D. Northrop (Eds.), *Health is academic: A guide to coordinated school health programs* (pp. 269–291). New York: Teachers College Press.

Hannaford, C. (2005). *Smart moves: Why learning is not all in your head.* Salt Lake City, UT: Great River Books.

Hanson, T. L., Austin, G., & Lee-Bayha, J. (2004). *Ensuring that no child is left behind: How are student health risks and resilience related to the academic progress of schools?* Retrieved from http://www.wested .org/online_pubs/hd-04-02.pdf

Health and learning. (2009). *Educational Leadership, 67*(4). Retrieved from http://www.ascd.org/ publications/educational-leadership/dec09/vol67/num04/toc.aspx

Health and physical education. (2004, Winter). *Curriculum Technology Quarterly, 14*(2).

Health education and physical education. (2002, Spring). *Curriculum Technology Quarterly, 11*(3).

Health, Mental Health and Safety Guidelines for Schools. (n.d.). *Family and community involvement.* Retrieved from http://www.nationalguidelines.org/chapter_full.cfm?chapter=family

Health, Mental Health and Safety Guidelines for Schools. (n.d.). *Health and mental health services.* Retrieved from http://www.nationalguidelines.org/chapter_full.cfm?chapter=mentalHealth

Health, Mental Health and Safety Guidelines for Schools. (n.d.). *Health and safety education.* Retrieved from http://www.nationalguidelines.org/chapter_full.cfm?chapter=health

Health, Mental Health and Safety Guidelines for Schools. (n.d.). *Nutrition and food services.* Retrieved from http://www.nationalguidelines.org/chapter_full.cfm?chapter=nutrition

Appendix

ASCD © 2010. All Rights Reserved.

Health, Mental Health and Safety Guidelines for Schools. (n.d.). *Overarching guidelines.* Retrieved from http://www.nationalguidelines.org/chapter_full.cfm?chapter=overarching

Health, Mental Health and Safety Guidelines for Schools. (n.d.). *Physical education.* Retrieved from http://www.nationalguidelines.org/chapter_full.cfm?chapter=physEd

Health, Mental Health and Safety Guidelines for Schools. (n.d.). *Physical environment and transportation.* Retrieved from http://www.nationalguidelines.org/chapter_full.cfm?chapter=physical

Health, Mental Health and Safety Guidelines for Schools. (n.d.). *Social environment.* Retrieved from http://www.nationalguidelines.org/chapter_full.cfm?chapter=social

Health, Mental Health and Safety Guidelines for Schools. (n.d.) *Staff health and safety.* Retrieved from http://www.nationalguidelines.org/chapter_full.cfm?chapter=staff

Healthy bodies, minds, and buildings. (2000). *Educational Leadership, 57*(6).

Healthy Schools Network. (n.d.). *Healthy schools network, inc.* [Home page]. Retrieved from http://www.healthyschools.org

Holt, S. A., Hale, G. E., & Murray, M. (2002). *Health and physical education: A chapter of the curriculum handbook.* Alexandria, VA: ASCD.

Holt-Hale, S. A., Ezell, G., & Mitchell, M. (2000). *Health and physical education: A chapter of the curriculum handbook.* Alexandria, VA: ASCD.

Institute of Medicine. (2009). *Local government actions to prevent childhood obesity.* Washington, DC: National Academies Press.

Johnson, A. J., & Breckon, D. J. (2007). *Managing health education and promotion programs: Leadership skills for the 21st century.* Boston: Jones and Bartlett Publishers.

Johnson, D. P. (2005). *Sustaining change in schools: How to overcome differences and focus on quality.* Alexandria, VA: ASCD.

Joint Committee on National Health Education Standards. (2007). *National health education standards: Achieving excellence* (2nd ed.). Atlanta, GA: American Cancer Society.

Kerns, J. T., & Ellis, R. E. (2003). *Health and safety guide for K–12 schools in Washington.* Retrieved from http://www.k12.wa.us/SchFacilities/Publications/pubdocs/CompleteSafety&HealthManual 2002-2003.pdf

Kessler, D. A. (2009). *The end of overeating: Taking control of the insatiable American appetite.* New York: Rodale Inc.

Kiernan, L. J. (Producer). (1997). *How to reduce stress in your school* [Videotape]. Alexandria, VA: ASCD.

Knoff, H. M. (2001). *The stop and think social skills program teacher's manual: Grades preK–8.* Boston, MA: Sopris West. Available from http://www.projectachieve.info/productsandresources/thestopthinksocial skillsprogramschool.html

Lambert, L. (2003). *Leadership capacity for lasting school improvement.* Alexandria, VA: ASCD.

Lambert, L. T. (2000). The new physical education. *Educational Leadership, 57*(6), 34–38.

Learning First Alliance. (2001). *Every child learning: Safe and supportive schools.* Alexandria, VA: ASCD.

Levi, J., Vinter, S., Richardson, L., St. Laurent, R., & Segal, L. M. (2009). *F as in fat 2009: How obesity policies are failing America.* Retrieved from http://healthyamericans.org/reports/obesity2009/Obesity 2009Report.pdf

ASCD © 2010. All Rights Reserved.

Appendix

Lewallen, T. C. (2004, August). Healthy learning environments. *ASCD InfoBrief, 38.*

Lohrmann, D. K. (2006). Process evaluation for school health professionals. *Journal of School Health, 76*(4), 154–155.

Lohrmann, D. K. (2008). A complimentary ecological model of coordinated school health promotion. *Public Health Reports, 123*(6), 695–703.

Lohrmann, D. K., & Wooley, S. F. (1998). Comprehensive school health education. In E. Marx, S. F. Wooley, & D. Northrop (Eds.), *Health is academic: A guide to coordinated school health programs* (pp. 43–66). New York: Teachers College Press.

Los Angeles County Office of Education. (2000). *Classroom management: A California resource guide.* (Available from Los Angeles County Office of Education, Safe Schools Center, 9300 Imperial Highway, Downey, CA 90242-2890)

Los Angeles Unified School District, Office of Environmental Health and Safety. (n.d.). *Model safe school plan: A template for ensuring a safe, healthy and productive learning environment.* Retrieved from http://www.lausd-oehs.org/schoolsafetyplans_v1.asp

Maguire, S. (2000). A community school. *Educational Leadership, 57*(6), 18–21.

Marx, E., & Checkley, K. (2003). *An ASCD professional development online course: Supporting student health and achievement.* Alexandria, VA: ASCD.

Marx, E., & Northrop, D. (1995). *Educating for health: A guide to implementing a comprehensive approach to school health education.* Newton, MA: Education Development Center.

Marx, E., & Northrop, D. (2000). Partnerships to keep students healthy. *Educational Leadership, 57*(6), 22–24.

McCloskey, M. (2007). The whole child. *ASCD Infobrief, 51.* Retrieved from http://www.ascd.org/publications/newsletters/infobrief/fall07/num51/toc.aspx

McKenzie, F. D., & Richmond, J. B. (1998). Linking health and learning: An overview of coordinated school health programs. In E. Marx, S. F. Wooley, & D. Northrop (Eds.), *Health is academic: A guide to coordinated school health programs* (pp. 1–14). New York: Teachers College Press.

McLeod, J., Fisher, J., & Hoover, G. (2003). *The key elements of classroom management: Managing time and space, student behavior, and instructional strategies.* Alexandria, VA: ASCD.

Miura, M. R., Smith, J. A., & Alderman, J. (2009). *Mapping school foods.* Retrieved from http://www.chefann.com/html/tools-links/cool-food-tools/mappingschoolfood.pdf

National Assembly on School-Based Health Care. (n.d.). [Home page]. Retrieved from http://www.nasbhc.org

National Association for Sport and Physical Education. (n.d.). *NASPE national standards.* Retrieved from http://www.aahperd.org/naspe/standards/nationalStandards/index.cfm

National Association for Sport and Physical Education. (2004). *Moving into the future: National standards for physical education* (2nd ed.). Reston, VA: Author.

National Association of State Boards of Education. (2009). *Partners in prevention: The role of school-community partnerships in dropout prevention.* Retrieved from http://www.nasbe.org/index.php/file-repository/func-startdown/1007/

National Association of State Boards of Education. (n.d.). *State school healthy policy database.* Retrieved from http://nasbe.org/healthy_schools/hs/index.php

ASCD © 2010. All Rights Reserved.

National Center for Chronic Disease Prevention and Health Promotion. (n.d.). *Health topics: Nutrition* [Home page]. Retrieved from http://www.cdc.gov/HealthyYouth/nutrition/index.htm

National Center for Chronic Disease Prevention and Health Promotion. (2007). *CDC's school health education resources (SHER): National health education standards (NHES)*. Retrieved from http://www.cdc.gov/healthyyouth/sher/standards/

National Center for Chronic Disease Prevention and Health Promotion. (2008). *CDC's school health education resources (SHER)* [Database]. Available from http://apps.nccd.cdc.gov/sher/

National Center for Chronic Disease Prevention and Health Promotion. (2008). *CDC's school health education resources (SHER): Characteristics of an effective health education curriculum*. Retrieved from http://www.cdc.gov/HealthyYouth/SHER/characteristics/index.htm

National Center for Chronic Disease Prevention and Health Promotion. (2008). *Physical education curriculum analysis tool (PECAT)*. Available from http://www.cdc.gov/HealthyYouth/PECAT/index.htm

National Center for Chronic Disease Prevention and Health Promotion. (2009). *Health education curriculum analysis tool (HECAT)*. Retrieved from http://www.cdc.gov/HealthyYouth/HECAT/index.htm

National Center for Chronic Disease Prevention and Health Promotion. (2010). *Nutrition, physical activity, and childhood obesity: Local wellness policy tools and resources*. Retrieved from http://www.cdc.gov/HealthyYouth/healthtopics/wellness.htm

National Center for Chronic Disease Prevention and Health Promotion. (2010). *School health policy*. Retrieved from http://www.cdc.gov/HealthyYouth/policy/index.htm

National Center for Chronic Disease Prevention and Health Promotion. (2010). *Strategies for addressing asthma within a coordinated school health program*. Retrieved from http://www.cdc.gov/HealthyYouth/asthma/strategies.htm

National Center for Chronic Disease Prevention and Health Promotion. (2010). *Student health and academic achievement*. Retrieved from http://www.cdc.gov/HealthyYouth/health_and_academics/index.htm

National Consortium for Physical Education and Recreation for Individuals with Disabilities. (1995). *Adapted physical education national standards (APENS)*. Champaign, IL: Human Kinetics.

National Diabetes Education Program. (n.d.). *Teens*. Retrieved from http://www.ndep.nih.gov/diabetes/youth/youth.htm

National Diabetes Education Program American Indian Work Group. (2006). *Move it! And reduce your risk of diabetes school kit*. Retrieved from http://www.ndep.nih.gov/media/moveit_school_kit.pdf

National School Boards Association. (2010). *Childhood obesity and schools* [Home page]. Retrieved from http://www.nsba.org/MainMenu/SchoolHealth/obesity-and-schools.aspx

National School Boards Association. (2010). *Search the school health database* [Database]. Available from http://www.nsba.org/MainMenu/SchoolHealth/SearchSchoolHealth.aspx

Nihiser, A. J., Lee, S. M., Wechsler, H., McKenna, M., Odom, E., Reinold, C., Thompson, D., & Grummer-Strawn, L. (2007). Body mass index measurement in schools. *Journal of School Health, 77*(10), 651–671. Retrieved from http://www.cdc.gov/HealthyYouth/obesity/BMI/pdf/BMI_execsumm.pdf

Novick, B., Kress, J. S., & Elias, M. J. (2002). *Building learning communities with character: How to integrate academic, social, and emotional learning*. Alexandria, VA: ASCD.

ASCD © 2010. All Rights Reserved.

Osorio, J., Marx, E., & Bauer, L. (2000). Finding the funds for health resources. *Educational Leadership, 57*(6), 30–32.

Paterson, K. (2007). *3-minute motivators: More than 100 simple ways to reach, teach and achieve more than you ever imagined.* Markham, Canada: Pembroke Publishers.

Physical and Health Education Canada. (2009). *Quality daily physical education* [Home page]. Retrieved from http://www.cahperd.ca/eng/physicaleducation

Quality counts 2008: Tapping into teaching, unlocking the key to student success. (2008). *Education Week, 27*(18). Retrieved from http://www.edweek.org/ew/toc/2008/01/10/index.html

Ratey, J. J. (2008). *Spark the revolutionary new science of exercise and the brain.* New York: Little, Brown and Company.

Reeves, D. B. (2009). *Leading change in your school: How to conquer myths, build commitment, and get results.* Alexandria, VA: ASCD.

Robert Wood Johnson Foundation. (2009, June). *RWJF research brief—Local school wellness policies: How are schools implementing the congressional mandate?* Retrieved from http://www.rwjf.org/files/research/20090708localwellness.pdf

Rogers, E. M. (2003). *Diffusion of innovations* (5th ed.). New York: The Free Press.

Rothstein, R., & Jacobson, R. (2006). The goals of education. *Phi Delta Kappan, 88,* 264–272.

Scherer, M. (Ed.). (2010). *Keeping the whole child healthy and safe: Reflections on best practices in learning, teaching, and leadership.* Alexandria, VA: ASCD. Available from http://shop.ascd.org/productdisplay.cfm?productid=110130E4

Schonfeld, D. J., Lichtenstein, R., Pruett, M. K., & Speese-Linehan, D. (2002). *How to prepare for and respond to a crisis* (2nd ed.). Alexandria, VA: ASCD.

School Nutrition Association. (n.d.). [Home page]. Retrieved from http://www.schoolnutrition.org

Seefeldt, V. D. (1998). Physical education. In E. Marx, S. F. Wooley, & D. Northrop (Eds.), *Health is academic: A guide to coordinated school health programs* (pp. 116–141). New York: Teachers College Press.

Shaps, E. (2003). Creating a school community: Building a strong sense of community in schools is both important and doable. *Educational Leadership, 60*(6), 31–33.

Smith, J. (2003). *Education and public health: Natural partners in learning for life.* Alexandria, VA: ASCD.

Strong, J. H. (2002). *Qualities of effective teachers.* Alexandria, VA: ASCD.

Sweeney, D. B., & Nichols P. (1998). The state role in coordinated school health programs. In E. Marx, S. F. Wooley, & D. Northrop (Eds.), *Health is academic: A guide to coordinated school health programs* (pp. 244–268). New York: Teachers College Press.

Tapping parent and community support to improve student learning. (2008). *Education Update, 50*(4). Retrieved from http://www.ascd.org/publications/newsletters/education-update/apr08/vol50/num04/toc.aspx

Taras, H., Duncan, P., Luckenbill, D., Robinson, J., Wheeler, L., & Wooler, S. (2004). *Health, mental health and safety guidelines for schools.* Retrieved from www.nationalguidelines.org

Teufel, J. A. (2006). An overview of school health center sustainability from an ecological perspective. *The Health Education Monograph Series, 23,* 24–29.

UCLA School Mental Health Project. (n.d.). [Home page]. Retrieved from http://smhp.psych.ucla.edu

ASCD © 2010. All Rights Reserved.

Resources

U.S. Department of Agriculture Food and Nutrition Service. (n.d.) *Local wellness policy*. Retrieved from http://www.fns.usda.gov/tn/Healthy/wellnesspolicy.html

U.S. Department of Agriculture Food and Nutrition Service. (2000). *Changing the scene: Improving the school nutrition environment*. Available from http://www.fns.usda.gov/tn/Resources/changing.html

U.S. Department of Agriculture Food and Nutrition Service. (2005). *Making it happen! School nutrition success stories*. Available from www.fns.usda.gov/tn/Resources/makingithappen.html

U.S. Department of Education. (n.d.). *Doing what works: Dropout prevention* [Home page]. Retrieved from http://dww.ed.gov/topic/?T_ID=24

U.S. Department of Education. (n.d.). *Education resource organizations directory*. Available: http://wdcrob colp01.ed.gov/Programs/EROD/org_list_by_territory.cfm

U. S. Environmental Protection Agency. (2010). *Healthy school environments resources*. Retrieved from http://cfpub.epa.gov/schools/index.cfm

Westbrook, J., & Spiser-Alberb, V. (2002). *Creating the capacity for change: An ASCD action tool*. Alexandria, VA: ASCD.

Wiley, D. C., & Howard-Barr, E. M. (2005). Advocacy to action: Addressing coordinated school health program issues with school boards. *Journal of School Health, 75*, 6–9.

Wilkinson, M. (2004). *The secrets of facilitation: The S.M.A.R.T. guide to getting results with groups*. San Francisco, CA: Jossey-Bass.

Wolfe, P., Burkman, M. A., & Streng, K. (2000). The science of nutrition. *Educational Leadership, 57*(6), 57–59.

Wooley, S. F., Eberst, R. M., & Bradley, B. J. (2000). Creative collaborations with health providers. *Educational Leadership, 57*(6), 25–28.

Zmuda, A., Kuklis, R., & Kline E. (2004). *Transforming schools: Creating a culture of continuous improvement*. Alexandria, VA: ASCD.

Healthy School Report Card
Expert Panel

Jacquee Albers, Education Consultant
Menands, New York

Angelo J. Bellomo, Director
Office of Environmental Health and Safety
Los Angeles Unified School District, California

John N. Boronkay, Assistant Superintendent
Manassas City Public Schools, Virginia

Beverly J. Bradley, Assistant Clinical Professor
University of California, San Diego Division of Community Pediatrics

Stephanie Bryn, Director
Injury and Violence Prevention, Maternal and Child Health Bureau
Health Resources and Services Administration, Rockville, Maryland

Joy Dryfoos, Board Member, Coalition for Community Schools
Institute for Educational Leadership, Washington, D.C.

Julia G. Lear, Director
Center for Health and Health Care in Schools, Washington, D.C.

Eva Marx, School Health Consultant
Hingham, Massachusetts

Erik Peterson, Director of Public Awareness
American School Food Service Association, Alexandria, Virginia

Eric Schaps, President
Developmental Studies Center, Oakland, California

Bela Shah, Program Associate, School, Family and Community Connections Program
Institute for Educational Leadership, Washington, D.C.

Bruce Simons-Morton, Chief, Prevention Research Branch
National Institute on Child Health and Human Development, Bethesda, Maryland

Julie A. Stauss Fort, Nutritionist
Child Nutrition Division—Food and Nutrition Service, U.S. Department of Agriculture,
Washington, D.C.

Judith S. Stavisky, Senior Program Officer
The Robert Wood Johnson Foundation, Princeton, New Jersey

Marlene Tappe, Professor, Health Education and Physical Education
Purdue University, W. Lafayette, Indiana

Howell Wechsler, Acting Director, Division of Adolescent and School Health
National Center for Chronic Disease Prevention and Health Promotion, CDC, Atlanta,
Georgia

Roger Weissberg, Executive Director, Collaborative for Academic, Social,
and Emotional Learning
Chair, Psychology Division of Community and Prevention Research, University of Illinois
at Chicago

Mark Weist, Executive Director, Center for School Mental Health Assistance
Professor of Psychology, University of Maryland–Baltimore

ASCD © 2010. All Rights Reserved.

Field Test Sites

Selma Middle School, Indiana

Shamrock Springs Elementary School, Westfield, Indiana

Slate Run Elementary School, New Albany, Indiana

Thomas Carr Howe Academy, Indianapolis, Indiana

FIELD TEST FACILITATOR

Suzanne Crouch
Indiana Department of Education, Indianapolis

ASCD © 2010. All Rights Reserved.

Appendix

Healthy School Community Pilot Sites

Barclay Elementary/Middle School
Baltimore, Maryland

Blackstone Academy
Pawtucket, Rhode Island

Boston Arts Academy
Boston, Massachusetts

Des Moines Municipal School
Des Moines, New Mexico

Hills Elementary School
Hills, Iowa

Thomas Carr Howe Academy
Indianapolis, Indiana

Iroquois Ridge High School
Oakville, Ontario

Orange County Schools District
Hillsborough, North Carolina

Pottstown School District
Pottstown, Pennsylvania

Appendix

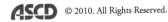 © 2010. All Rights Reserved.

Healthy School Community Pilot Sites

Queen Elizabeth Secondary School
Surrey, British Columbia, Canada

Woodland Park Elementary
Surrey, British Columbia, Canada

ASCD © 2010. All Rights Reserved.

Appendix

About the Author

David K. Lohrmann is a professor of applied health science at Indiana University, Blooming-ton. His expertise includes school health programs, prevention education, program evaluation, and education reform. He also serves as a consultant for the Michiana Coordinated School Health Program Leadership Institute, which is sponsored by the Great Lakes Chapter of the American Cancer Society, the Indiana State Department of Health, and the Michigan Department of Education. Lohrmann was previously director of the Evaluation Consultation Center at the Academy of Educational Development and director of curriculum for the Troy School District in Michigan.

His article "A Complementary Ecological Model of the Coordinated School Health Program," initially published in *Public Health Reports* (2010) and subsequently in the *Journal of School Health* (2010), provided the first reconceptualization of this approach in more than 20 years. Additionally, he coauthored *Comprehensive School Health Education* in the book *Health is Academic: A Guide to Coordinated School Health Programs*, published by Teachers College Press (1998).

Lohrmann, who holds a doctorate in health education from the University of Michigan, is a fellow and former president of the American School Health Association. He received the William A. Howe Award in 2009 from the American School Health Association in recognition of career professional service and the Scholar Award in 2010 from the American Association for Health Education for career scholarly productivity.